○

Anyone interested in how Buddhism was established in the West should appreciate the efforts of the numerous individuals, some both brilliant and flawed, whose exertion and compassion benefit all practitioners. Shishin's honest and compelling memoir arises from his experiences at the center of many of those efforts. He has shared a wonderful and personal journey.

—Charles G. Lief, president, Naropa University

The path of the first generation of American Zen students is fascinating, and Shishin Wick's memoir is an important contribution to that history.

—David Loy, author of *Money, War, Sex, Karma: Notes for a Buddhist Revolution*

This was a fascinating read. It's well written and very engaging—and as an insider I enjoyed the behind-the-curtain perspectives on so many of the important developments of Zen in America that Shishin was right there to witness.

—Josh Bartok, abbot of the Greater Boston Zen Center and editorial director, Wisdom Publications

Apart from this memoir being something like a one-man history of Zen in America, with his intimate knowledge of so many of the different figures, Shishin's approach to teaching and practice has an honest and authentic feel to it.

—Dave O'Neal, senior editor, Shambhala Publications

○

My American Zen Life

O

Gerry Shishin Wick

ISBN 978-0-9763016-3-9

Available for purchase at Lulu.com

Published by Scrivana Press

Eugene, Oregon, and Iowa City, Iowa

Make a searching analysis of yourself. Realize that your body is not your body. It is part of the whole body of sentient beings. Your mind is not your mind. It is but a constituent of all mind.

—Soyen Shaku, "First Step in Zazen"

CONTENTS

9   *Acknowledgments*

11   *Chapter 1*   WHY ZEN?

22   *Chapter 2*   WHAT IS?

36   *Chapter 3*   FROGGY AND THE ROCK OF GIBRALTAR

42   *Chapter 4*   GRANDMOTHER ZEN

55   *Chapter 5*   ON THE ROAD

70   *Chapter 6*   JAPAN

80   *Chapter 7*   FORK IN THE ROAD

94   *Chapter 8*   UPHEAVAL

110   *Chapter 9*   BACK TO LAY LIFE

121   *Chapter 10*   SAYONARA JAPAN

131   *Chapter 11*   GREAT MOUNTAIN ZEN CENTER

145   *Chapter 12*   SHINKO

159   *Chapter 13*   MAITREYA ABBEY

172   *Chapter 14*   WHITE PLUM ASANGA

185   *Chapter 15*   NEW DIRECTIONS

200   *Chapter 16*   BEARING WITNESS

Acknowledgments

The influences of many people shaped *My American Zen Life* and my American Zen life. First I offer many deep bows of gratitude to my Zen mentors: Maezumi Roshi, Sochu Roshi, and Roshi Bernie Glassman. I am especially indebted to the women who agreed to share their lives and the Zen path with me. I have learned more from Ilia Shinko Perez, Julie Doju Robbins, and Marsha Burack than they could imagine. I have always enjoyed and appreciated the support of my siblings, Alan, Barry, and Barbara.

My Zen life has been especially enriched by my wife and Dharma partner Shinko Perez. I have also been enriched through interactions over the decades with many of my Dharma brothers and sisters too numerous to mention. Nonetheless, I individually acknowledge the contributions of Joko Beck, Chozen Bays, Seisen Saunders, Egyoku Nakao, Enkyo O'Hara, Bill Henie, Daido Loori, Genpo Merzel, Jikyo McMahon, Myoyu Andersen, Yuin Hamilton, Tenshin Fletcher, Michael Taizen Soule, Genmyo Smith, Jissan Christensen, Genro Gauntt, Genki Kahn, Eve Marko, Sally Tanshin Rorick, Father Robert Kennedy Roshi, Peter Kakuzen Gregory, Margi Teido Gregory, and Romulo Sanchez.

I also thank all of my students. Some have remained loyal, some have left in a huff, some fluctuated in their devotion, and others just wandered away. I love you all.

Lastly but not finally, I thank Jessie Dolch, who did an amazing job of editing and fact checking the manuscript. I accept responsibility for all errors as my memory has a limited capacity. I also thank Niki Harris for the wonderful layout and cover design. There would be no book without them.

The vast majority of the photos in the book came from my personal archives and the archives of the Zen Center of Los Angeles. Other photos were taken by Peter Cunningham (p. 141), Marsha Steckling (p. 157), Lisa Schaewe (pp. 169 and 190), and Paul Agostinelli (cover photo). The calligraphy on the cover is my full Dharma name written by Maezumi Roshi, who also carved the cover stamp with my Dharma name. The stamp on the back cover represents the Three Treasures of Buddha, Dharma, and Sangha.

Finally, deep gratitude to my children, Sam, David, Dan, and Lily, and my step-daughter Janna, for putting up with all of my idiosyncrasies and absences while I vigorously followed my Zen path. You have remained loyal in spite of it all.

Chapter 1

WHY ZEN?

Unmon asked the monks, "At the sound
of the bell, why do you put on your robes
and come to the meditation hall?"
—*Gateless Gate* Case 16

I am often asked, "What got you into Zen?" Somehow I
always had an answer, and now after fifty years of Zen practice,
I am not so sure I believe myself. We do all kinds of things in
our lives, some of them admirable and some of them hurtful.
Then after the fact, we rationalize and justify our actions to try
to make some sense of them.

Through my Zen training, I learned that it is impossible to
logically answer a question that starts with the word "Why." I
spent twenty-five years studying Zen koans, with several Zen
masters. Koans are often described as logical paradoxes used
to liberate the minds of Zen students. The epigraph above is a
Zen koan. "At the sound of the bell, why do you come to the
meditation hall?" "At the sound of the bell, why do you enter
the classroom?" "Why did you buy a Volvo instead of a BMW?"
"Why are you marrying her?" "Why Zen?"

Back in the 1970s there was a self-improvement craze called
est (Ehrhard Seminars Training). At the end of the introductory

course, the trainer showed the participants two imaginary ice cream cones and told them, "Here is a chocolate and a vanilla cone; choose one." When you chose, you were asked, "Why chocolate?" or "Why vanilla?" If you answered, "I like chocolate" or "I hate vanilla," your answer was not accepted. Only one answer indicated that you took in the intent of the training. You chose chocolate because you chose chocolate!

So, why Zen?

So many conditions gave rise to our lives as they are. We never know all of the factors that determine what we do. But we have our stories, and the stories inform us and can inspire others. When I started to study Zen, I found that stories of those who preceded me encouraged me to continue despite my resistance and confusion. In that spirit, here is my story—My American Zen Life.

But at the same time, it is not just my life. As Soyen Shaku says in the epigraph to this book, your body and mind are not just yours; they are part of the whole body, of all mind. My life is not just my life; it is also your life. And your life is also my life.

○

I have always been a seeker. As a young boy, when I was told that God created everything, I was the one who asked, "Who created God?" I was raised Jewish but never lived in a close Jewish community. I was born in 1941, four months before the United States entered World War II. My father joined the military and was stationed near Las Vegas, Nevada. The only other Jews in Las Vegas during the 1940s were the American mobster Bugsy Siegal and his cohorts. We were Jews surrounded by Gentiles. In all of the places we lived during my childhood, there were very few Jews. We stood out. I started elementary school in Las Vegas; finished it in Sherman Oaks, California; and attended middle and high school in Phoenix, Arizona.

In about the second grade, I realized that I was different from the other kids. For one thing, they celebrated Christmas. We did not. I recall the feelings of loneliness and alienation that arose for me on Christmas morning—especially when I saw my friends riding new bikes or playing ball with new baseball mitts.

Mother did her best to make Hanukah a festive occasion for our family. She baked holiday sweets and decorated the house with Stars of David and Menorahs. We lit the candles each night and the kids got presents. But I just wanted to blend in and not be different.

After we moved to California, my brother Alan and I had to go to religious school in North Hollywood on Saturdays— the Jewish Sabbath. Aside from my reactions to the school, Saturday is the day for Little League baseball. But because of the Sabbath religious school, we had to miss opportunities to join and play.

Besides such practical frustrations associated with school on Saturdays, I found some of the Bible stories that we read in religious school to be very frightening. Everyone drowned in the flood that carried Noah's ark—even innocent children. When God killed the firstborn son of every Egyptian family to allow the Jews to escape slavery, my joy at the liberation of the Jews was tempered by my sorrow at the deaths of the innocent Egyptian boys. My child's mind reverberated with conflict and confusion. Why would God be so mean? Would he kill me if I wandered from the straight and narrow? It was horrible!

When we moved to Phoenix, all of the Jews lived in the northwest quadrant of town. But we lived in the southeast, so again, I was surrounded by Gentiles. From my classmates in the seventh grade I learned that "Jew" was a verb and not a very pleasant one at that. I also learned that the Jews had killed Jesus and that I was personally responsible. It was a big cross to bear for an eleven-year-old.

In fact, I hated all of my Jewish education. I studied Hebrew at the Temple Beth Israel for two years after regular school and attended religious school until I was sixteen. I had to take the bus and transfer to get home. I viewed this as a severe imposition that must have been a punishment from God. I challenged and deprecated my teachers and even got expelled, but Mom and Dad made me apologize, and I got reinstated—much to my chagrin.

Despite my disconnection from my Jewish education, I excelled in regular school. I loved it and wanted all of the accolades I could get. But every year I had to miss school because of the Jewish High Holy Days—Rosh Hashanah and Yom Kippur. The services were so tedious I thought I would die and be eaten by dogs. And when they gave out awards for perfect attendance at elementary school, I always lost out because of the High Holy Days.

I never found a rabbi who inspired me. I needed to find meaning about why I was Jewish, and my thirst for a connection with the transcendent or God or the mysterious unknown always went unsatisfied.

At about the age of twelve, I unconsciously determined that if I had to be Jewish, I needed some heroes. Moses did not cut it. He got too angry when the Jews worshipped the Golden Calf after he descended Mount Sinai with the stone tablets. Abraham was out because he was prepared to kill his son Isaac as a sacrifice to show his faith to God. So I had to turn to sports, the arts, science—or even organized crime. There were some pretty cool guys in the Jewish mafia who did not take shit from the Gentiles.

Eventually, I settled on Albert Einstein as my hero. Maybe that had something to do with my chosen field of study in physics. Upon reflection, I think I went into physics in order to satisfy my quest for ultimate reality—which I did not find in Judaism. Later I discovered Zen Buddhism.

Ironically, I was around more Jews at the Zen Center of Los Angeles during the 1970s than at any other time in my life. We even celebrated the Passover Seder there. But those JuBu's—Jewish Buddhists—just wanted to get drunk on the many glasses of wine and cared less about the service. What kind of Jews are those? It is interesting to me that many Jews became Buddhists. Now I am a JuBu myself.

In 1962 I graduated with honors in physics from Pomona College and was accepted into the Ph.D. program at the University of California, Berkeley. I reconnected with a high school friend, Marsha Burack, who transferred to Berkeley from Antioch College via Arizona State University. Marsha was bohemian, artistic, sensual—and intellectually curious about physics. I was conventional, a scientist, and an athlete—having competed in football and swimming during college. On the surface we had little in common other than our roots in the Jewish community in Phoenix. Nonetheless, we felt a strong attraction and got married in the summer of 1963. If not for Marsha, I probably would have followed the conventional middle-class path of my parents. She opened me to new ways of viewing the world and helped me to chart a new course for my life.

The 1960s were exciting times in Berkeley—a time of big social, political, and personal changes. We were exposed to everything. I was enthralled by talks by civil rights activist Malcolm X, Manhattan project director J. Robert Oppenheimer, right-wing segregationist Major General Edwin "Ted" Walker, physicists Edward Teller and Richard Feynman, anthropologist Ashley Montagu, and many more. We attended concerts by Thelonious Monk, Otis Redding, Nina Simone, Charlie Mingus, Bob Dylan, and Joan Baez. And then there were the drugs, the Beatles, and rock music.

One of the big changes in my life involved drugs. In 1964, Marsha's cousin Wally Sheffey stayed with us at our apartment in Berkeley and introduced us to LSD. (Wally later changed his name to Womapati Das after joining the Hare Krishnas.) I loved it. Every trip was a good trip. Amazingly, most of my trips had a religious element to them. Good Jew that I was, I had many visions involving Jesus and the cross. Such experiences helped me see that my version of reality was very tenuous. A few micrograms of a psychedelic substance could completely

Marsha, me, and my brother Barry in Berkeley, 1966

alter how I saw the world. And it was much more beautiful and mysterious than I had previously experienced it to be. Some of my friends were overwhelmed by terror during their LSD trips and swore it off. But I found every LSD experience fascinating, even the unanticipated journeys into the netherworlds.

In the broadway play "The Search for Signs of Intelligent Life in the Universe," Trudy the bag lady, played by Lily Tomlin, says, "Reality is nothing but a collective hunch." That is not so far from the observation of the science historian and philosopher Thomas Kuhn in his book *The Structure of Scientific Revolutions*. He concluded that scientific truth is what those scientists in power say is scientific truth and that when they die and a new generation of scientists assumes the reins of power, scientific truth changes.

I continuously pondered what was real and what was not real. I thought that physics was real and that through my studies I would find the answers to my questions about the source of everything. But the more I studied physics, the more I found questions rather than answers. After years of contemplation and study, I concluded that physics obviously advances knowledge, but it provides no closure. Rather than behaving like a circle that closes on itself, physics was more like a torus or spiral that advances but never finds closure. To paraphrase a famous aphorism from Einstein about mathematics, I found that as far as the laws of physics referred to reality, they were incomplete, and as far as they were complete, they did not refer to reality.

$$\mathbf{\Omega}$$

The next year, just as it was published, I came across a copy of *The Three Pillars of Zen*, the first book written about Zen practice. There had been many books about Zen *philosophy*, such as those by Alan Watts and D. T. Suzuki, but this book, compiled by Philip Kapleau, had stories of enlightenment experiences and the paths followed by Zen practitioners. I was taken by a particular enlightenment experience that turned out to be that of Koun Yamada, whom I later met in Japan after he became a Zen master, or Roshi.

Yamada Roshi was reading the following phrase from a seventeenth-century Zen text: "I came to realize clearly that Mind is no other than mountains and rivers and the great wide earth, the sun, the moon, and the stars." Suddenly the bottom dropped out of his fixed perceptions, and he deeply comprehended this statement. He cried and laughed uncontrollably and told his wife, "In my present exhilarated frame of mind I could rise to the greatest heights."

Subsequently I took LSD with my brother Alan, climbed up a tree, and continuously repeated the line, "I came to realize clearly that Mind is no other than mountains and rivers and the great wide earth, the sun, the moon, and the stars." I was exhilarated, and we both rose to the greatest heights. But after ten hours, the feeling disappeared and I was faced with my school work, an argument with Marsha, and our dirty flat. Right then I decided that I could be high, have transcendent experiences of unity with the divine, and experience the extraordinary beauty of the world without drugs by learning how to meditate. And I thought that I would never have to come down. Wrong!

Marsha and I bought *zafus* and *zabutons* (Zen meditation cushions) and converted a small room in our flat into a meditation room. We tried to sit meditation without any instruction other than what we found in *The Three Pillars of Zen*. It was difficult, both physically and mentally. Because I was an athlete, my muscles were hard and inflexible. My knees, hips, and back started to scream at me if I sat still in the Zen posture for more than ten minutes. Trying to quiet my mind was almost impossible. I had spent my life to that point accumulating intellectual knowledge and using my brain power to solve abstract problems and to direct my life. The gears were always engaged. Trying to tap into the subtle wisdom of my body was like a mosquito trying to bite an iron bull.

○

In the 1960s Zen Master Shunryu Suzuki was becoming well-known in the Bay Area. He arrived from Japan in 1959 and founded the San Francisco Zen Center, which was on Bush Street. I recall going to a free rock concert in the panhandle of Golden Gate Park that featured the Grateful Dead, Jefferson Airplane, Country Joe and the Fish, and Suzuki Roshi. Between sets, Suzuki Roshi sat cross-legged on the stage and spouted Zen wisdom in his broken English. At least I thought it was wisdom. I could not understand what he was saying because his English was so encrypted. If I did manage to decrypt it, his words were totally enigmatic. However, his presence was so engaging and his laugh and smile so infectious that Marsha and I decided to join him at Bush Street for *zazen* (seated Zen meditation).

The San Francisco Zen Center in 1966 was in a former Jewish synagogue that had been converted into a Japanese community center. The *zendo* (meditation hall) was in front of an auditorium that must have been the sanctuary. We would meditate for twenty to thirty minutes, and then Suzuki Roshi would give a talk and take questions. Probably no more than a dozen people attended. What caught my attention was that a few of my fellow white Americans could sit cross-legged on their cushions with their backs straight in perfect posture without moving for the entire meditation period. I was constantly squirming and fidgeting. But I did have one small advantage. From the age of twelve to nineteen, I was a competitive swimmer. I practiced many hours in the pool regulating my breathing to coordinate with the arm strokes and to improve my performance. Breathing is one of the three elements of Zen practice, along with disposition of the body and disposition of the mind. Even though my body and mind rebelled during zazen, I was still a champion at breathing. As my Zen practice matured, it was my breathing that allowed me to penetrate to the depths of my mind and to quiet my restless body.

About halfway through the Zen center program, a Japanese youth band would start their rehearsals in the auditorium. The band usually rose to its climax as Suzuki Roshi started to speak. Again, I hardly understood anything he said, but I got from him that this life is precious and we should not waste it. I felt determined to continue on my spiritual path, and Suzuki Roshi was an inspiration that nudged me in the right direction.

$$\bigcirc$$

Later that year Marsha's brother, Richard Burack, moved to Berkeley to enter a graduate program in psychology. He had just graduated from Stanford University. Richard was also taken by Zen, drugs, and rock and roll. In 1967 he joined the Berkeley Zendo, which was run by Mel Weitsman, a senior student of Suzuki Roshi. In the summer of 1967, Tassajara, the first Zen monastery in the United States, was opened for rigorous Zen training. Tassajara was founded by Suzuki Roshi in the rugged mountains near Santa Cruz, California. Richard was selected to participate in the first training period.

I completed all of the requirements for my Ph.D. in physics that same summer. I finished my dissertation under the direction of Professor Eugene Commins on "Test of Time Reversal Invariance in the Beta Decay of Neon-19." Heady stuff. We were attempting to determine whether the laws of physics are valid independent of whether time runs forward or backward. Before a committee of five professors, I successfully defended my dissertation, which showed that time flow did not matter at the level of elementary particles—at least to the accuracy of our measurements. All I needed was the piece of paper that said I was a Ph.D. from the University of California, Berkeley. In the meantime, I had several offers of jobs in the field. Ultimately, I wanted to teach physics at a small liberal arts college similar to Pomona College where I had gotten my bachelor's degree. But I had an offer to do nuclear physics research at the British Atomic Energy Research Establishment about an hour west of London. Since I had not been to Europe and had the wanderlust of youth, I chose to go to England, thinking I could always come back and get a teaching job. Wrong!

Before packing up and trekking to Europe, Marsha and I, accompanied by our sister-in-law Susan Wick, spent a week at Tassajara at the invitation of Richard. By coincidence, years later, Susan traveled to Japan and met a Zen priest, Kosen Nishiyama, who was translating the *Shobogenzo*, the most famous work of the most famous Japanese Zen master, Eihei Dogen. Susan cleaned up his English and got a credit as a translator, although she admits that she did not understand most of Dogen's profound writings.

At Tassajara, we sat meditation, learned to use *oryoki* bowls (Zen eating bowls), soaked naked in the magnificent hot pools, and lay in the sun while the trainees were doing their tasks. Since it was the first monastic training in the United States, they were taking it seriously. But it seemed too rigid and harsh to me. It was only much later that I learned how rigorous Zen training is. And I also found out how much joy there can be in this serious practice.

Chapter 2

WHAT IS?

> When Seppo was living in a hut, two
> monks came to pay respects. Seeing them
> coming, Seppo pushed open the door of
> the hut, popped out, and said, "What is
> it?" A monk also said, "What is it?" Seppo
> hung his head and went back inside.
> —*Blue Cliff Record* Case 51

Marsha and I drove across country from Berkeley to New York in the late summer of 1967 to catch our flight to Europe. We camped in the natural beauty of the West and visited Berkeley friends in Minnesota; my sister Barbara, who was a student in Madison at the University of Wisconsin; Marsha's relatives in Chicago; family friends in Cleveland; Amish country in Pennsylvania; and ended up staying with my brother Barry, who was a student at Columbia University.

I had never been to New York City. We explored much of Manhattan. We even walked down 125th Street at night to the Apollo Theater in Harlem to hear Martha and the Vandellas. Fortunately, we were so stoned that we were not frightened at being the only whites on the street and in the theater.

The highlight of my trip was taking acid in the

Metropolitan Museum of Art. I spent most of my time in the Asian collection staring at the large Buddhas. In my altered state, I heard the most beautiful, celestial music in that room. I was transported to the Tushita heaven, where one day is equivalent to four hundred years, and I drifted in space with all of the Buddhas and bodhisattvas. I kept thinking that this must be nirvana.

On the bus ride home from the museum, every person I looked at was the Buddha. I kept telling Barry and Marsha that there were Buddhas everywhere in New York City. We would see a fat man who looked like he was chewing his cud, and I would tell Barry, "There is the Buddha." We would see a bag lady, and again I would say, "There is the Buddha." Later I learned that upon awakening, the Buddha said, "Everyone without exception has the wisdom and virtue of the Buddha." But, the Buddha continued, "They do not realize it due to their attachments and deluded thoughts." When I seriously started to practice Zen, I learned more about attachments and deluded thoughts than I ever wanted to.

Marsha and I flew from New York in September and landed in Paris. We rented a car and spent the next two months driving around France and Germany and went through the Austrian Alps to Yugoslavia and Greece. Then we took a ferry to Italy where we drove the peninsula from south to north, traversed Switzerland, and arrived back in Paris. Everywhere we went we sought out the mystical artworks of medieval and Renaissance Christianity. I especially resonated with Giotto's murals in the Arena Chapel in Padua showing everyone in prayer with their eyes raised to the heavens, and the huge paintings of Rubens in Der Alte Pinakothek in Munich. Much of the art gave us contact highs and helped us connect with the divine. We also got high, literally, when we pilgrimaged to

Jim Morrison's gravesite in Paris. I never could have thought then that years later I would be in the home of his fellow Doors musician Ray Manzarek, who was interested in Zen.

We crossed the English Channel and arrived at Victoria Station in London and then went on to the Atomic Energy Research Establishment in Harwell. There, I did nuclear physics research while Marsha tried to entertain herself in an environment that was very remote from Berkeley.

There was no Zen in the English countryside of Berkshire County at that time. There were, however, a lot of Hindus who immigrated to England from India, and we sampled their spiritual fare. We attended meditative gatherings, or *satsangs,* and kirtan chant groups, and my scientific mind rebelled at all of the magic and emphasis on faith in things that I could not see or hear and that made no sense to me.

After two years, we were ready to leave Harwell. Marsha wanted to return home. I did get an offer from Cal Tech in Pasadena, but I also got one from CEA Saclay, the French nuclear research facility outside of Paris. I chose Paris, which ended up being a difficult prospect for Marsha. She had a nervous breakdown that left us stranded in London.

There I was in a foreign country—without money, without a job, and with a wife who could barely function. I thought it was terrible, but everything turned out much better than I could have imagined at the time. Marsha gradually recovered, and I eventually got a great job. Furthermore, Sochu Suzuki Roshi, a Zen master from Japan, showed up in London.

○

Looking at it in retrospect, my situation reminds me of the Taoist story of Mr. Sei and the horse. Mr. Sei lived in a small village with his horse. Because he had a horse, Mr. Sei was one of the wealthiest villagers. His neighbors would tell him how lucky he was to have that horse. Now he could plow a much larger field, have a much larger income, and take much better care of his family. But Mr. Sei was a wise man. He didn't say anything; he just nodded his head.

One day the horse ran away. Then Mr. Sei's neighbors told him how unlucky he was that his horse had run away. Mr. Sei said nothing. Not commenting, he just nodded his head in acknowledgment of the situation.

Then the horse returned—followed by a second horse. Mr. Sei's neighbors then told him how lucky he was that his horse had run away because now he had two horses. Again Mr. Sei said nothing and simply nodded his head, acknowledging the state of things.

Meanwhile, his son was plowing the field with the second horse, and he had an accident and broke his leg. The neighbors told Mr. Sei how unlucky he was to have that second horse because his son had broken his leg and couldn't help in the fields.

Then a war broke out in the province and the lords conscripted all the young men to fight. But Mr. Sei's son had a broken leg and couldn't go to battle. So the neighbors told Mr. Sei how lucky he was that his son had broken his leg . . .

And so it goes. We have so many ideas about how things *should* or *could* be. The truth is that we never know how things will turn out. True freedom is being able to make the best of things *as they are.*

O

I searched around and eventually landed a job at *New Scientist* magazine writing popular articles about physical science. I wrote hundreds of articles about physics, chemistry,

geology, and astronomy in the three years I worked there.
Marsha was getting better when we heard about Sochu Roshi.
He was invited to teach at the Buddhist Society in Eccelston
Square by Christmas Humphries, the society's president. Sochu
Suzuki was the abbot of Ryutakuji Monastery located on the
slopes of Mount Fuji in Japan. He was the senior disciple of
Soen Nakagawa, one of the early Zen masters to visit the United
States, and he was the senior Dharma brother of Eido Shimano
Roshi—one of the several Zen teachers who has recently been
condemned for his abuse of power with women in his Zen
communities in New York state.

Christmas Humphries introduced Sochu Roshi to a large
crowd at his first meeting at the Buddhist Society. After the
attendees realized that Sochu Roshi wanted everyone to sit
in meditation and not just listen to him talk about Zen, the
subsequent meetings dwindled to a handful. After a few weeks,
Sochu indicated in his limited English that he wanted to leave the Buddhist Society and teach Zen to those who wanted to put their bodies on the line and practice. He puffed himself up and said that those who ran the Buddhist Society thought they knew about Zen, but they only knew how to

Sochu Roshi, 1970

talk about it.

One of Sochu's students was an older man named Magnus Wechsler who had some financial means. He provided a place for Zen practice and brought in a bunch of younger people from a Gurdjieff group that he ran. Sochu assigned everyone to work on the famous koan Joshu's Mu:

> A monk asked Joshu in all earnestness, "Does a dog have Buddha Nature or not?" Joshu answered, "Mu."

We had to sit with that Mu, which literally means "no" or "not," and penetrate into the intent of Joshu. Conceptually, Joshu is demonstrating Buddha Nature, which is the essence of everyone and everything. I spent the next six years trying to penetrate that "gateless gate" set up by Master Joshu.

During this visit Sochu spent a year in London. We meditated every day, and once a month we had an intensive period of meditation, called *sesshin*, which lasted from two to five days during which we sat eight or nine hours in meditation daily. Sochu held the space for everyone and performed all of the zendo functions. He gave talks (which were translated since

London sesshin with Sochu (on the left), 1971. I am sitting to Sochu's left.

his English was almost nonexistent), he gave private instruction to each student (called *dokusan*), he led the chanting and played all the traditional instruments, and he prepared all the meals and taught us how to use the oryoki bowls and to eat mindfully.

If I sat more than thirty minutes in a day, my body screamed at me and implored me to stop. "Why are you doing this to me?" it would ask in despair. But intermittently, something amazing would happen. My mind would become quiet and I would feel spacious and calm. The pain in my legs would disappear. At first, this might happen only once during a two-day sesshin. Then it would happen twice or three times and last for more than a minute or two. My scientific mind told me that perhaps the Buddha and Zen masters were telling the truth. This was a way to the home I yearned for. Meditation started to become like an addictive drug. Yet I still suffered. Sometimes when Sochu Roshi was in the kitchen preparing a meal, I would get up and go to the bathroom just to stretch my legs. On occasion, I would run into him as he was returning to the zendo, and he would raise his eyebrows—but would not browbeat me.

Sochu's attempts at English were often endearing. I recall that he confused "kitchen" and "chicken." Later I realized that those two words have the same sounds, but in opposite order—like a phonetic anagram.

Almost every week, I took Sochu out and about in London. As we walked along, he would point at this and that and say, "What is?" A car would go by—"What is?" A traffic light would blink—"What is?" It would start to rain—"What is?" Everything was "What is?" Once he made a beautiful calligraphy of an *enso,* a Zen calligraphic circle, and wrote *ABCDCBA* under it. Then he asked, "What is?" I said,

"Letters." He said, "Not letters, what is?"

In the epigraph to this chapter, Seppo asks, "What is it?" Later in the same koan, his Dharma brother Ganto answers by saying, "Just this." Ganto said "Just this" more than a thousand years ago. Zen students have repeated his words over and over until they have become a hackneyed phrase like that of the monk in our epigraph who repeats Seppo's "What is it?" Until one has totally experienced "Just this," they are merely dead, conceptual words. Sochu was looking for the live expression from me.

○

Sochu returned to Japan after a year in London, leaving our small group, or *sangha,* of about a dozen people on its own. The mother of one member of our group owned a small import shop in the Soho district in London's West End. We set up a zendo there in the basement and took turns opening it each morning for zazen.

Marsha and I had a flat in Maida Vale in northwest London. On the mornings when it was my turn to open the zendo, I got up in the dark and walked to Edgware Road to catch the No. 6 bus to Soho. Sometimes, three of four of us would be there, but more often than not, I was the only one. The basement was cold, dank, and musty. On cold winter mornings, condensed moisture collected on the walls and formed small rivulets as gravity drew it toward the center of the earth. Yet, I fulfilled my duties and rang the meditation bells and sat the requisite time.

There is a phenomenon that can occur during Zen meditation called *makyo,* which means illusion or hallucination. During zazen, the room can become brilliantly white or pitch black. Or one's body can feel like it is floating or is so heavy it is sinking into the earth. Patterns on the walls and floor can give rise to makyo by oscillating or creating bizarre images. The dank walls of our basement zendo with the moisture popping up could give rise to the makyo of nightmares. As a veteran of many LSD trips, I took makyo in stride, but some people became frightened and wanted to quit meditating. Others mistook makyo for an enlightenment experience and insisted that they had deep insight when white light appeared. They needed a good Zen teacher to tell them to forget it and get back on their cushion.

Later I learned that makyo occurs when one's concentration deepens but the three elements—body, mind, and breath—are not quite in harmony. In the beginning I had many makyo, but they subsided and disappeared with time.

○

In the summer of 1969, when I was twenty-eight years old, my father died in Phoenix of a heart attack. I did not have enough money to fly there for the funeral. After I heard the news and talked to my mother on the phone, I wandered around London asking myself, "Where is my father now? Where is my father now?" Hindus and Buddhists talk about reincarnation, but I had no proof of that. Many years later, I worked on this koan:

> If you realize your own nature, you certainly are free from life and death. When your eyes are closed, how can you be free from life and death? If you are free from life and death, you know where you will go. When the four elements are decomposed, where do you go? (*Gateless Gate* Case 47)

Now I believe that reincarnation is possible, but my understanding of life and death does not depend on it. With each breath we die and are reborn. If our mind is pure and clear, we can awake to the eternal life where nothing is extra and nothing is lacking. It is not easy, but it is possible and takes tremendous determination, faith, and continual deep soul searching.

$$\bigcirc$$

London was an exciting place when we lived there. Through Zen, I met Leon Redler, a New York psychiatrist who was an integral part of R. D. Laing's radical psychiatry at Kingsley Hall. Leon and I became good friends and he introduced me to "Ronnie" Laing and other members of the Philadelphia Association, such as Joe Berke. The anthropologist Francis Huxley, a member of the well-known Huxley clan, was part of that group. He brought to London a famous peasant Shaman named Arrigo, who performed impressive surgeries with a rusty knife. The spirit flowed through Arrigo and while in a trance, he cured serious illnesses. My scientific mind was reeling.

Through my job at *New Scientist,* I made contact with many important scientists of the day. Marty Perl, who later won the Nobel Prize in physics, was on sabbatical leave from Stanford University, and we became fast friends. I hung out with Willie Fowler, another future Nobelist, who was on leave from Cal Tech. He introduced me to Fred Hoyle, the major proponent of the steady state theory of the universe as opposed to the Big Bang.

Through my physicist friends, I was offered a part-time post at Birkbeck College of the University of London to teach nuclear physics. I taught there for two years and was able to spend time with David Bohm, a senior faculty member who contributed unorthodox and innovative ideas to the field of quantum physics. He was a pioneer in developing a holographic view of the brain and of the world. Bohm spent considerable time with the Indian philosopher and mystic Jiddu Krishnamurti and studied both Hinduism and Buddhism and brought them into his scientific views.

○

Near the end of 1970, Marsha became pregnant. We had talked about returning to the States to live, and we took a trip there in early 1971 to see our families and to look for a job. It was our first trip back in more than three years.

One of our stops was Berkeley, where Richard was still practicing at the Berkeley Zendo. One morning I joined them for zazen and Suzuki Roshi showed up. I pounced at the opportunity and invited him to London to teach our sangha there. I had no idea when or whether Sochu Roshi would return, and I felt the need for a teacher, any teacher, even though Sochu practiced in the Rinzai Zen tradition and Suzuki Roshi in the Soto tradition. Suzuki Roshi looked at me and laughed. I took that as a no. Little did I know that he was sick with cancer and would die later that year.

In koan Case 87 of the *Book of Equanimity* Sozan goes to Isan with a question about the Dharma and Isan laughs. Later Sozan understands Isan's laughter and says that there was a sword in his laugh. That sword is the sword that cuts off delusion. Suzuki Roshi's laugh might have had a sword, but I was still as deluded as ever.

Marsha and I returned to London with no job prospects in the States. The job climate had changed for physics professors, and I had to look elsewhere. Fortunately I had made a connection with Professor John Isaacs of the Scripps Institution of Oceanography in La Jolla, California, and he was interested in my diverse background. We corresponded for a year, and he eventually offered me a job as an oceanographer.

Back in London, I started to look again for a Zen teacher. Jiyu Kennett Roshi, an Englishwoman who had studied in Japan, was holding programs in Surrey south of London. I went to see her a few times before she immigrated to the United States and founded Shasta Abbey in Mount Shasta, California.

I heard about the Friends of the Western Buddhist Order run by the Venerable Sangharakshita, an English army officer who had studied in India and Southeast Asia and been ordained by a Burmese Buddhist monk. I loved his retreats. In addition to meditation we had exercises to release our emotional attachments. In one exercise, we stared into the eyes of a partner and watched the judgments and resistance that arose. Much later other Buddhist teachers in the United States did similar things.

I heard about the Tibetan Buddhist teacher Chögyam Trungpa Rinpoche, who had a monastery called Samye Ling in Scotland, but I did not have the time or money to visit him. We did meet years later in Los Angeles after he had moved to the United States and started training programs in Boulder, Colorado.

Then, Sochu contacted us and decided to send Katsuki Sekida to live in London and lead our fledging Zen group. Sekida-san, as we called him, was a retired English teacher who had studied Zen with Soen Nakagawa Roshi and Sochu Roshi. He made it clear that he was not a Zen master but that he was willing to give us talks about Zen and to sit with us. Sekida-san was in his late sixties although he seemed older. He went on to write two well-regarded Zen books in English, *Zen Training:*

Sekida-san with my son Sam, 1971

Methods and Philosophy and *Two Zen Classics: The Gateless Gate and The Blue Cliff Records.*

On July 16, 1971, Marsha's and my twin sons, Samuel Bodhi and David Sochu, were born in London. I could no longer take a leading role in our sangha, and Marsha pretty much dropped out. But I did continue to participate in almost all of the Zen programs.

Sochu Roshi returned to London shortly before New Year's in 1971. With Sekida-san translating, we could begin to understand the subtleties of his teachings. Previously, his main teaching had been "Sit! Sit! Sit!" We had several sesshin, and I vividly recall one in a house where the only private room for dokusan was the bathroom. And it was a small bathroom. We entered and did our prostrations to the commode and then turned to the left where Sochu Roshi sat in the shower stall. He was the most unpretentious man. I described him as having his head in the clouds and his feet on the ground.

○

In 1972 the offer came to me from Professor John Isaacs to return to the States and work as an oceanographer at Scripps. As we were preparing to move, Marsha told me that she had fallen in love with another man and was going to remain in London with the twins. I was crushed but had committed to the new job and was ready to leave England. Then Sochu invited me to accompany him to New York on my way back and to join him at a seven-day sesshin that he was going to co-lead with Eido Shimano.

My head spun with conflict and confusion, and it was with deep sadness that I bade good-bye to Marsha and our babies and boarded the plane at Heathrow to fly toward the next phase of my life.

Chapter 3

Froggy and the Rock of Gibraltar

> A monk asked Unmon, "How do Buddhas
> appear?" Unmon answered, "The eastern
> mountain walks along the stream."
> —*Collection of Vines and Entanglements*
> Case 57

My brother Barry was still living in New York City when
I arrived at the end of winter 1972. During the intervening
five years since I had last seen him, he had graduated from
Columbia University and had started living at the Integral Yoga
Institute, where he was a secretary to Swami Satchidananda
and had married Padma, another student at the institute.
Everyone called him Siva, his new yogic name. He had become
a strict vegetarian and continues that diet today.

Barry took me to the Zen Studies Society on East 67th
Street where I met Sochu Roshi and Tai-san, as we called Eido
Shimano then. Tai-san was not yet a Zen master or Roshi, but
it was clear that he was in charge. Sochu and Tai-san were a
study in contrasts. Sochu was more a patched-robed, simple
monk. Tai-san wore fur-covered boots and a fur hat with neatly
pressed Zen priest's clothes that had a sheen. He conveyed the
air of being dashing and modern. Sochu had no pretenses.

All of the assembled students boarded a bus that took us for a couple hours' ride to Litchfield, Connecticut, to a home for retired Catholic nuns where the sesshin was to be held. About thirty people must have attended the weeklong retreat. We were placed in the zendo according to seniority, with the men starting on one side and the women on the other. The two rows met in the middle. Since my seniority was undefined, I sat at the end of the men's row between a man of low seniority and a woman who was at the end of the woman's row.

The woman was a beautiful young lady named Sherry Nordstrom. She was married to Lou Nordstrom, who was also at the sesshin. Lou, a Buddhist scholar, later became a successor of Bernie Glassman, my Dharma brother and mentor, and Sherry is now Shinge Roshi, the abbot and spiritual director of the Zen Studies Society and a Dharma successor of Shimano Roshi.

When the Buddha seated himself beneath the Bodhi tree before his enlightenment experience, he made the following resolve: "Let only skin, sinew, and bone remain, let the flesh and blood dry in my body, but I will not give up this seat without attaining complete awakening." The Litchfield sesshin was my first seven-day sesshin. I had sat for five days but had not sat still for the entire time. When the bell rang signaling the beginning of this sesshin, I made the following resolve: "I will not fidget, change my position, or move during any sitting period for these seven days." Tai-san did not make it easy.

In the morning we got up at 4 a.m. and joined a line of meditating walkers who followed a path in the nunnery along the Stations of the Cross. It did not escape me that I was walking up Mount Calvary to my own crucifixion.

The length of the sitting periods was pretty predictable with Sochu Roshi. We sat about thirty minutes, and then did

Tai-san (Eido Shimano), 1972

walking meditation for ten minutes, and then another thirty minutes of sitting, and so on. Tai-san, however, varied the length of the sitting periods. Sometimes they were twenty minutes long, and sometimes they lasted one hundred minutes. When we sat down we did not know when the bell would ring to signal the end of the sitting period. I felt like I was entering Dante's Inferno: "Abandon all hope, ye who enter here." I had no option but to put myself totally into my zazen.

Tai-san leads great sesshin. He gave a series of Dharma talks, or *teisho,* on various koans. His English was clear and articulate, so I had a sense of understanding what he was talking about. The zazen was strenuous much of the time. My legs and mind kept telling me to bolt and run with abandon into the snowy woods that surrounded the nunnery. But I remembered my vow not to move or fidget. At times, the body would break into a profuse sweat or I had to grit my teeth against the pain. Then it would happen: I suddenly would be floating in space with no pressure on any of my joints. My body disappeared and I felt like I was drifting between the stars. I was the space. I was the stars. All pain and suffering had evaporated. Where it went, I did not know, and I did not care because I could breathe again and feel the breath pass through my body like the wind through the trees.

I was always aware of everything that was happening in my body and mind. That awareness reassured me that there was a huge subjective element to pain. If I could only relax and allow the pain to wash over my body, I would experience these moments of bliss more often. Sure, who are you kidding? In the next moment the pain would return with a vengeance. It went up and down like this for the entire seven days.

Every day, Tai-san held dokusan with the students. When the bell rang signaling the beginning of dokusan, the students stampeded to get in line to see him. I went about every other day. I was still struggling with the koan Mu, and Tai-san would look at me and pat me on the shoulder and say, "Not yet, not yet!"

Every day during the afternoon break, Sochu Roshi and I would take a walk along a snowy path in the woods. He was particularly interested in what happened with me in dokusan. Mostly we would walk, and he would encourage me to keep doing my best. I was his only student at the sesshin, and he was acting like a mother hen.

On about the fifth day of sesshin while we were doing walking meditation, or *kinhin*, Tai-san had us chant "Enmei Jukku Kannon Gyo," a short Japanese chant about finding the Buddha and Bodhisattva of Compassion, during all activities throughout the day. The sounds were meaningless, but we chanted them over and over. Tai-san encouraged us to chant louder and louder. It seemed that this went on for a long time. When we finally stopped, I was as high as I had ever gotten from smoking the best Moroccan hashish. And just like a pot high, it faded away in time.

Finally, it was the last day, the last hour, and the last minute of sesshin. At the end was a ceremony called the Great Release, or Dai Kaijo. And it did feel like a great release. I felt like steam that escapes from a pressure cooker. Everything was light and airy and radiant.

As I was packing up, I saw the fellow who sat next to me and thanked him for his support. He looked at me and said in his New York accent, "Boy was I pissed at you!" I was startled and asked, "Why is that?" He said, "You were making so much noise with your breathing, I started to call you 'Froggy.' But then I got used to it and it was okay." I apologized for disturbing his meditation and went to find Sherry Nordstrom to apologize to her.

But Sherry said, "Are you kidding? You sat like the Rock of Gibraltar." In that moment I wondered who they were talking about. In the epigraph above, Unmon is asked, "How do Buddhas appear?" He appears as Froggy sitting on my left croaking on his lily pad. She appears as the Rock of Gibraltar on my right, solid and immovable. With every searing pain in my legs, a lotus flower appeared, and on that lotus flower sat a Buddha. The eastern mountain walks along the stream.

I felt like bringing my sitting partners together and saying, "Froggy, I would like you to meet the Rock of Gibraltar. Rock of Gibraltar, this is Froggy." I was only the conduit, the mirror, and a blank sheet of white paper.

Everyone was milling around and engaging in animated conversation. I was standing on the side, and Sochu Roshi walked up to me and swung his arm and opened his hand as if he were throwing confetti into the air. Then he said, "Samadhi going away fast." *Samadhi* is the power of concentration. It is said that samadhi is the precursor to enlightenment. During a weeklong sesshin, one can develop considerable samadhi power. Sochu wanted me to look after it and maintain it well.

As I boarded the bus to return to New York City, Sochu said good-bye. I saw him only one more time before he died—about four years later at Ryutakuji in Japan where he was abbot.

I vividly remember that bus ride. I noticed the new leaves

on the trees, the reflection of the sun off the small streams along the way, the billowing clouds that seemed alive; even the noise and congestion of New York City had its charm. The feeling stayed with me for days. My sesshin in Litchfield was a turning point in my life and my practice. I now knew that there was no turning back. Zen was my path.

Chapter 4

GRANDMOTHER ZEN

> You can understand all of Buddhism, but
> you cannot go beyond your abilities and
> your intelligence unless you have *robai-*
> *shin,* grandmother mind, the mind of
> great compassion.
> —Eihei Dogen, *Eihei Shingi*

I arrived in San Diego on April Fool's Day 1972. What a contrast from London! The sky was blue, the air was warm and fresh, and flowers bloomed in profusion. If you wanted to see flowers in London, you had to go to Regent's Park in the spring and summer. Here, flowers showed their faces all year round. In April the succulents along the highways displayed bright purple flowers that stretched for miles. There were huge commercial fields of ranunculus that radiated reds, purples, yellows, and oranges.

The Scripps Institution of Oceanography is located on the enchanted La Jolla Cove. I sat for hours entranced by the waves and the cliffs. I truly had landed in the Western Paradise.

Before leaving New York I had asked Tai-san about any Zen contacts he had in San Diego, and he referred me to Ray Jordan, a professor of religious studies at San Diego State University.

Ray had practiced Zen with Nyogen Senzaki, one of the Zen pioneers in the United States, and with Soen Nakagawa, who was the teacher of Tai-san and Sochu Roshi.

Ray hosted an evening of zazen in his home every Wednesday evening. I immediately joined and looked forward to sitting with the small group that gathered there. Ray was very stiff and formal. Everyone entered in silence and took their places on the cushions. After we had sat for two periods, Ray would read from a typewritten manuscript of talks given by Nyogen Senzaki on the *Gateless Gate,* the most famous collection of koans. Then Ray would formally serve Japanese tea in silence, and when we finished we were all ushered out of the house onto the front porch. If anyone exchanged words, it was while loitering on the front porch with the other Zen students.

About thirty years later, I was at a gathering with Eido Roshi (or Tai-san) and casually mentioned the Nyogen Senzaki manuscript. Eido's eyes got as big as saucers, and he asked whether I could get a copy for him. I just happened to have a copy that I had made from Ray Jordan's original. The talks were finally published in 2008 in the volume *Eloquent Silence: Nyogen Senzaki's Gateless Gate and Other Previously Unpublished Teachings and Letters,* edited by Sherry Roko Chayat (who is the same Sherry Nordstrom who manifested as the Rock of Gibraltar in Litchfield), with a foreword by Eido Shimano. I am happy to say that I am the link that helped bring this Zen treasure to the public.

The students who gathered with Ray Jordan seemed to be either older women or young men. The first person to approach me was a tall, blond, handsome fellow named Bill Henie. Bill's aunt was the famous Sonja Henie, who won three Olympic gold medals in figure skating for Norway and then turned her fame into a Hollywood career. Sonja had died without children in 1969 and left much of her fortune to Bill's family. He lived with his mother and brother in a beautiful house in Oceanside on a large plot of land called Henie Hill.

Bill told me that some of the Zen students were studying at the Zen Center of Los Angeles with Taizan Maezumi Roshi and that I ought to go there with him for a sesshin. I eventually was able to do that and to meet Maezumi Roshi. When I met him, Maezumi Roshi threw out a baited line and I bit—and ended up studying with him for twenty-three years.

One of the older women was a devoted student of Maezumi Roshi. When we got around to talking, I learned that Charlotte Joko Beck was not only engaging, but also worked at the University of California in San Diego where I worked. She was the administrative assistant in the chemistry department, and I was a research physicist in the oceanography department. We arranged to meet with our sack lunches on the campus and continued to meet weekly for the next five years until she moved into the Zen Center of Los Angeles.

After eating our lunches, we took long walks and discussed the vagaries of Zen. As I often saw her do, Joko would stare intensely ahead and poke her finger at the air in front of her while exclaiming, "This is not real." She had recently had a

Maezumi Roshi, 1980

"big" experience in a sesshin with Yasutani Roshi, and she kept telling me that "it was horrible." Yet she was more determined than ever to deepen her understanding.

Joko met Maezumi Roshi in 1966 at a Unitarian church she attended in San Diego. She knew nothing about Zen and admitted that she did not understand much of what he said, but when he stood at the door and looked each person in the eye and bowed to them as they exited, she saw something that compelled her to start practicing zazen.

I do not know exactly the age at which Joko started to sit. It was most likely when she was fifty. She would meet with a few other women her age and sit zazen for five minutes and then talk for an hour about how difficult it was. Joko never enjoyed sitting or attending sesshin. I often repeat what she once told me: "There is only one thing worse than attending sesshin—*not* attending sesshin!"

On our walks, Joko often talked about the death of Shirley Syson, one of the middle-aged women in Joko's group who seemed to embody the heart of Zen before the rest of them. Joko was present at Shirley's death and was greatly impressed by Shirley's radiance and peace even as cancer consumed her body. I believe that experience was the prime moving force for Joko's practice. Later, Shirley's widower, John Syson, hosted weekend sesshin for our little San Diego sangha, which Maezumi Roshi attended.

Joko and I arranged to have Maezumi Roshi come to San Diego for a weekend sesshin at a house I was renting in La Jolla. We planned everything, from the meals to procuring all the ritual implements, such as bells and clappers and a wooden percussion instrument often shaped like a fish called a *mokugyo*. When it came time for the chanting service, we had only a bell. I still smile when I think of Joko beating out the

Joko and me at ZCLA (after we had both ordained with Maezumi Roshi), 1980

rhythms on a thick phone book using a large wooden spoon as our makeshift mokugyo. The *umpan,* a gong rung at meal time, was a pot lid that we struck with a large metal spoon. When the toilet gave out from overuse, we all scurried down to the corner gas station to use the bathroom there.

Joko had an intellectual curiosity about anything that helped her make sense of her Zen experiences. Since I was trained in physics, she often wanted to talk about quantum mechanics. She pored over a book by Hubert Benoit titled *The Supreme Doctrine* (later reissued as *Zen and the Psychology of Transformation*). She kept insisting that I read it, and every time I tried, my mind rebelled. She found that it explained some of the things she was going through and gave her a way to express it to others. Her youngest child, Brenda (Chiko), told me that it was one of three books that Joko always kept nearby and often reread throughout her life.

Once she saw the benefits of zazen, Joko was relentless in pursuing her practice. Every Saturday she would drive two hours to the Zen Center of Los Angeles for dokusan with Maezumi Roshi, and then she would drive two hours back home. Joko would put a "Do Not Disturb" sign on her bedroom door when she was meditating, and her four children knew better than to bother her. In order to spend time with Joko, Brenda started sitting when she was thirteen and attended her first sesshin when she was fourteen.

In 1974 when Brenda left home to attend college, Joko had an empty house. By that time, I was going through a divorce with Marsha, and Joko asked whether I wanted to rent a room. We lived together for a year until I found a place on the beach. Every morning we sat zazen and continued weekly sittings at Ray Jordan's house. Under different circumstances, we easily could have had an abiding love affair. But as it was, she, at age fifty-seven, was to me, at age thirty-two, the personification of Grandmother Zen. She had *robai-shin,* grandmother mind. She was tough and loving at the same time, but always with a compassionate heart. Joko was my best Dharma friend. We maintained contact until her death in 2011.

$$\bigcirc$$

One evening, Soen Nakagawa, Sochu's teacher, turned up at Ray Jordan's house. He was in town to lead a sesshin, which unfortunately I could not attend. I did have a chance to visit with him and told him how I was trying to do my best in Zen practice. Soen said, "Try? Try?" Of course I was trying, and he was acting as if I didn't need to try. Isn't effort, or *virya,* one of the *paramitas,* or aspects of the enlightened person? Isn't "Right Effort" one of the steps on the Eightfold Path as taught by the Buddha?

This is a common conundrum that beginning Zen students share. If I don't make an effort, how am I going to awaken? If I do make an effort, how do I know that I am putting my energies in the right direction so that I don't miss the mark? In Case 43 of the *Gateless Gate,* Master Shuzan holds up his staff, showing

Soen Roshi, 1974

it to the assembled disciples, and says: "If you call this a staff, you are stuck to the name. If you say it is not a staff, you deny the fact. Tell me, what do you call it?"

While pondering these questions, I came across a copy of *Hsin-Hsin Ming* (Affirming Faith in Heart/Mind), a long poem written by the Third Zen Patriarch in China in the sixth century. One line in particular stood out for me: "Do not seek for the truth; just cease to cherish your opinion." He was giving a prescription about how to practice Zen. I did not have to make an effort to find enlightenment; I just needed to make an effort to let go of my attachments and deluded thoughts.

I recalled part of a soliloquy I had memorized in college from Shakespeare's *Henry IV, Part 1,* spoken by Prince Hal:

... herein will I imitate the sun,

Who doth permit the base contagious clouds

To smother up his beauty from the world,

That, when he please again to be himself,

Being wanted, he may be more wonder'd at,

By breaking through the foul and ugly mists

Of vapours that did seem to strangle him.

The truth is like the sun that is obscured by the clouds of delusion. It is always shining, but the clouds of our fixed beliefs hide it from view.

I wrote the line "Do not seek for the truth; just cease to cherish your opinion" on an index card and posted it on my bulletin board at work. Every time I looked at it, I was reminded that I did not have to try to be enlightened. I just needed to get rid of whatever I was holding onto that was extra. The state of enlightenment is sometimes described as "Nothing lacking and nothing extra." I needed to work on this from both ends. I felt I was lacking something and did not yet know how to reveal what it was. But I could pare down my attachments to reach the state of "nothing extra." It came to me that "Right Effort" is getting rid of whatever is extra, including cherished opinions, deluded thoughts, and harmful actions.

Around that time, Bill Henie and I went on a camping trip to Ojai, California, to hear a public talk by the Indian teacher Krishnamurti. We bumped into Ray Jordan, who actually smiled at us—and his face did not break into pieces and fall off! It seems that Ray had a Zen persona and a different persona for the other parts of his life. In my Zen journey I am sorry to say that I have met too many Zen students and Zen teachers who have not carried their lives into their practice or their practice into their lives. What is that about?

Krishnamurti's talk about enlightenment and liberation and being free from conditioning was very inspiring. When someone asked him how to realize these states, he said, "Just do it." Where is the owner's manual for enlightenment? "Just do it" is too terse. But I was able to get some clearer instruction on the Zen path.

○

Meanwhile, my life went on. After I left London, Marsha remained there for a year before returning to the United States. I was able to visit about three times to see her and Sam and David, who were one year old. My sadness at being separated from my family did not abate. Zen was the touchstone that kept my life steady, but during that first year in San Diego, I would get stoned many evenings, put Pink Floyd's "Dark Side of the Moon" on the stereo, lie on the couch, and cry for hours.

My work at the oceanographic institute was interesting and exciting and diverted me from my sadness. Professor John Dove Isaacs was one of the most imaginative and brilliant men I had ever met. He and his wife, Mary Carol, took me under their wing. They had four grown children who were about my age, and they included me in their lives.

Physics was such a highly developed field of study, it took years of training to be able to make any contribution. In contrast, there were many simple and obvious unsolved problems in oceanography. I collaborated with Professor Isaacs in the realms of ocean engineering, biological oceanography, and physical oceanography. Most of my effort went to studying how to get renewable energy from ocean waves and from salinity gradients. I eventually wrote and edited a book called *Harvesting Ocean Energy*

Professor John Dove Isaacs, 1978

(1981), published for government policymakers by the United Nations.

Professor Isaacs was interested in the "deep scattering layer," a large community of marine animals that migrate daily from the ocean depths to near the surface and back. There was debate about whether their movement was triggered by circadian rhythms or by sunlight. In 1973 a total solar eclipse was to occur, and Professor Isaacs sent me and one of his assistants, a gregarious Turk named Sargun Tont, to the Atlantic Ocean to take measurements during the eclipse. We discovered a Greek luxury liner that was taking passengers to view the eclipse, and they labeled the cruise as a scientific voyage. Since it was much cheaper to book passage on the ocean liner than to take an oceanographic research vessel, we just needed to persuade the captain to let us lower our instruments during the voyage. Not only did they support our research, but they wanted us to be part of the show for the passengers. They already had booked Scott Carpenter, the astronaut, and Roger Tory Peterson, the birding expert and a well-known meteorologist. We just had to give a presentation to the passengers as part of their program and explain what we were doing. The experiment went well, and we decisively showed that the eclipse disturbed the movement of the deep scattering layer, which put a dent in the circadian rhythm theory. This was my one and only cruise on a luxury liner. I felt like I was in an episode of the TV series *The Love Boat,* as there were plenty of attractive women onboard who were interested in science—and in a mystical oceanographer. My loyalty to Marsha had ebbed with the tide.

Professor Isaacs and I, with two graduate students, caused quite a stir in the scientific community with a paper we published in the prestigious scientific journal *Nature* about automobile traffic creating tornadoes. We got thirty years of data from the National Climatic Data Center and mapped the occurrence of tornadoes in the United States. Two patterns in the data stood out: tornadoes were increasing with time, and the incidence of tornadoes was lowest during the weekends, exhibiting a seven-day cycle. One of our critics said that you might as well correlate tornadoes with X-rated movies since tornadoes need hot, steamy air. We had better criticism of our own work and were able to refute all detractors until everyone lost interest. As Professor Isaacs said in our defense, in all of the world's literature, there is only one reference to natural phenomena that have a seven-day cycle, and that occurs in the Book of Genesis.

As part of my training at Scripps, I took a master scuba diving course and went for numerous dives. I have always loved swimming in the ocean, and scuba was a special treat. I could go on about all of the interesting places I dove and strange experiences I had, but one stands out. A few hundred yards off the beach at Scripps, the sea floor is cleaved in a number of places by submarine canyons that precipitously drop to the abyssal deep. When one swims along the sea floor from the shore to the open sea, the bottom suddenly drops off into a dark gaping maw. If a swimmer is not careful, the currents that flow down the canyon walls can pull him or her a thousand leagues below. Floating over the canyon mouth, I felt a scary unity with the cosmos. It is the closest thing I can imagine to taking a space walk as an astronaut, which was my secret dream.

On another project, Professor Isaacs and I with another graduate student were developing an apparatus that would allow a deep-sea diver to remain warm. We were testing it in a tank that was about forty feet deep that had cold ocean water continuously circulating through it. I was a subject in the tests. With probes all over my body, I went to the bottom of the tank while my core body temperature, blood pressure, and other variables were measured.

While I was floating near the bottom of the tank, I thought of Case 43 in the *Blue Cliff Record*, "Tozan's Hot and Cold":

> A monk in all earnestness asked Master Tozan, "How do you avoid the discomfort of hot and cold?" And Master Tozan said, "Go to that place where there is no hot and cold." And the monk said, "Where is that place?" And the Master said, "When you are hot, be hot, and when you are cold, be cold."

When you are cold, be cold. Since I was not wearing a wet suit, it was very cold. I asked myself, "What's cold?" I totally experienced the cold. With each breath my whole universe was a feeling of cold penetrating my whole body.

Most of the subjects had to leave the water after twenty minutes because their body temperature dropped too low. But I stayed there, concentrating on the cold, and after an hour I was finally told to come up. My body temperature had barely dropped. The naval officer who was running the tests asked me, "What were you doing down there?" I replied, "Nothing." I imagined that if he knew, the navy would classify meditation as top secret. After that experience I didn't get cold for the longest time. I really understood "Tozan's Hot and Cold."

The apparatus we developed delivered warm moist air to the diver's lungs. Professor Isaacs figured that most body heat was lost through the lungs, but the navy's program, called the Hot Wet Suit program, relied on keeping the skin warm. Although our apparatus worked quite well, it did not fit into the Hot Wet Suit program and did not receive further support. Professor Isaacs called that phenomenon "the tyranny of the first successful solution."

I have seen the tyranny of the first successful solution at work in my life and the lives of others. When the circumstances of life change, we still cling to our old habits and ways of behaving that no longer serve us. Zen Master Hakuin, who lived in Japan in the eighteenth century, said that our "habit-ridden consciousness" holds back the development of our meditation practice more than anything. As my Zen practice matured through the years, Hakuin's words rang truer and truer.

Chapter 5

ON THE ROAD

> Joshu asked Nansen, "What is the Way?"
> "Ordinary mind is the Way," replied
> Nansen. "Shall I try to seek after it?" Joshu
> asked. "If you try for it, you will become
> separated from it," responded Nansen.
> "How can I know the Way unless I try
> for it?" persisted Joshu. Nansen said,
> "The Way is not a matter of knowing or
> not knowing. Knowing is delusion; not
> knowing is confusion. When you have
> really reached the true Way beyond doubt,
> you will find it as vast and boundless as
> outer space. How can it be talked about on
> the level of right and wrong?" With these
> words, Joshu came to sudden realization.
> —*Gateless Gate* Case 19

Zen students from San Diego put many miles on Interstate 5 that runs along the coast from San Diego to the Zen Center of Los Angeles (ZCLA). It is a one-hundred-mile trip and takes two hours when the traffic cooperates. I took my first trip with Bill Henie in September 1972 to attend a three-

ZCLA with zendo on right and sangha house on left, 1978

day sesshin that started on a Thursday evening. At that time ZCLA owned two houses on Normandie Avenue between 9th Street and San Marino Street. At its peak ten years later, the center owned seven houses and four apartment buildings on the same square block.

The neighborhood was rough. ZCLA is located in the Koreatown section of Los Angeles, but Normandie Avenue was populated with a mixture of Koreans, Hispanics, and low-income whites. Drugs were openly sold on the street corners and in a small park behind the center. The streets were dirty and smelled of urine. It was not unusual to hear gunshots and police helicopters hovering overhead during zazen. Normandie Avenue was the dividing line between the Rampart and Wilshire police precincts. If you called to report a crime, the desk sergeant would ask which side of the street it was on. Then he or she might refer you to the other police precinct, even if someone's life was being threatened.

I remember my first meeting with Maezumi Roshi as being

very sweet. He was kind and encouraging. He knew Sochu Roshi and was pleased that I had had some previous training. He spoke quite good English. He encouraged me to continue working on Mu, which I did. Since I was one of the older students (a mature thirty-one years old) and was professionally established, Roshi had me sleeping on the floor in his apartment during sesshin. After the initial dokusan, he pushed me to penetrate further into Mu, and his demeanor became tougher and tougher.

Maezumi Roshi had been empowered by teachers in both of the major Zen lineages, Soto and Rinzai. The Soto school is the school of meticulous practice and silent illumination. It emphasizes proper zazen, which will eventually lead to awakening. In contrast, the Rinzai school is more vigorous and uses koans to push the Zen student beyond his or her conceptual mind directly to awakening. Roshi, as we all called Maezumi Roshi, was born into a family of Soto priests. His father, Baian Hakujun, was a high official in the Soto school, and Roshi received Dharma transmission from him—that is, was established by him as a teacher in the Soto lineage. All of the ritual forms that we adapted at ZCLA were from the Soto tradition. As a student Roshi lived in the dojo of Koryu Osaka Roshi, a lay Rinzai teacher. Roshi studied koans with Koryu Roshi and eventually received *inka*, or sanction as a Roshi, from him. While in Los Angeles, Roshi translated for Yasutani Roshi, who came from Japan to teach. Yasutani Roshi was the main protagonist in the book *The Three Pillars of Zen*, which had initially raised my interest in Zen. Yasutani was a Soto priest who integrated the strong points of both Soto and Rinzai in a unique school, Sanbo Kyodan (now called Sanbo Zen), started by his teacher Harada Daiun Sogaku. Maezumi Roshi started to study with Yasutani and traveled to Japan to finish his studies

Maezumi Roshi with his parents, Baian Hakujun and Mrs. Kuroda, 1972

and be sanctioned again as a Roshi. When I met him, Maezumi Roshi has just completed his studies and was empowered by both Koryu and Yasutani.

Roshi was a very elegant man. He was an excellent calligrapher and Japanese gardener. He had a great aesthetic sense. He was precise and mindful of order and knew how to effectively interact with all kinds of people. But all of that changed when he got drunk.

Many of his students used to think that the "real" teachings came when Roshi was drunk. He dropped all pretenses, said what was on his mind, and acted spontaneously regardless of the consequences. Since I was a commuter to ZCLA, I saw this side of Roshi only after sesshin. A number of us would gather around him in his kitchen while he drank and offered drinks to the assembly. Then he would start probing individuals.

He would say to me, "Ask me!" I never knew what to ask him. If I said, "What should I ask?" He would again say, "Ask me!" If I said, "What is the best way to enlightenment?" or some other pompous Dharma question, he would stick out his tongue and make a farting sound. And thus it would go on.

One time when we were alone and quietly drinking in his apartment, he said something that touched a deep nerve in me. I started to sob and Roshi said very affectionately, "That is what I have been waiting for." He saw my protective armor and rigidity and kept working at breaking them down. In the dokusan room, that was his main objective with me for the first few years I studied with him.

In retrospect, it is clear that his close students were enabling Roshi's drinking and, as it turned out, his womanizing. In some ways, we were like a dysfunctional family. And it all came to a head about ten years later in the mid-1980s. (We will get to that story shortly.)

For six years while I lived in San Diego, I attended almost every sesshin at ZCLA. At first, they were three-day sesshin that started Thursday night and went through Sunday dinner. I usually drove there with Joko. We would pack our sesshin gear, meet right after work, and start driving. We usually arrived just as the *han* (wood block) was being struck, signaling the beginning of sesshin. We would park the car and run into the zendo in order not to be late. I had to take a vacation day every month on Friday, and I took almost all the rest of my annual vacation going to sesshin. In about 1974 ZCLA started to have seven-day sesshin on a regular basis, and those took a big bite out of my vacation time. When I would return back to work, Professor Isaacs without fail would ask me, "How was your séance?"

As the years passed, more Zen students from San Diego started to make the trek to Los Angeles. At Ray Jordan's house

I meet two professors of ecology, Michael Soule and Richard Etheridge. They both attended sesshin at ZCLA and started to bring in others. I drove Michael's wife, Jan, to her first sesshin. She was a natural and became a favorite of Maezumi Roshi. After Michael and Jan's divorce, Jan remarried and is now Jan Chozen Bays, co-abbot of Great Vow Monastery in Oregon with her second husband, Laren Hogen Bays. Richard introduced Zen to two of his nieces, Karen and Ann, who both moved to ZCLA. Karen later married Elihu Genmyo Smith, who studied many years with Maezumi Roshi and eventually became a successor of Joko's.

The cars that made the circuit from San Diego to ZCLA carried a bevy of future Zen teachers: Joko, Jan Chozen Bays,

ZCLA sangha after sesshin, 1975. Tetsugen was head monk. Front row (*left to right*): Maezumi Roshi, Tesshin Sanderson (now teaching in Mexico City), Tetsugen, Bishop Yamashita from Zenshuji in LA, and Maezumi's brother Kojun. Another brother, Junyu, is standing at the end of a row directly above Kojun. John Daishin Buksbazen in on the far left; behind him is a pouting Genpo Merzel. Robert Joshin Althouse (now teaching in Chicago) is behind Tetsugen. Brenda Chiko Beck with the long hair is in front of the pillar, top left, and Joko is just below her to her left (partially obscured). I am in the top row, right, between Jim Jimyo Culnan and Bill Nyogen Yeo.

Anne Seisen Saunders, Susan Myoyu Andersen, Elizabeth Yuin Hamilton, and me—the divine feminine and me. Eventually, all of us moved to ZCLA for a while and then dispersed, carrying seeds of the Dharma to the four winds.

Nansen said, "Ordinary mind is the Way." Ordinary mind is the mind of our everyday lives. We just drove for two hours to sit zazen and then drove two hours back to clean our houses, do our laundry, and get ready for work. I heard that Joshu Sasaki Roshi from Cimarron Zen Center (now Rinzai-ji Zen Center) in Los Angeles would ask his students, "How do you realize your Buddha Nature while driving on the Los Angeles freeway?" Driving two hours to study with our teacher was what we naturally did without question. Twenty years later, when I was teaching in Boulder, Colorado, we found a property that we could afford for our Great Mountain Zen Center about twelve miles away in the commuter town of Lafayette. The drive from Boulder took twenty minutes, but it nonetheless posed a serious barrier for about half of my students. Much to my amazement, they quit coming. When I compare the hardships of my Zen training with the stories of the ancient masters, they pale in comparison. Yet, few students today seem to be willing to give everything away to the practice like we did.

O

If Maezumi Roshi was the heart of ZCLA, his senior disciple, Bernie Tetsugen Glassman, was the mind of the operation. Tetsugen, who now prefers to be called Bernie, was a Ph.D. engineer and mathematician. He worked in the aerospace industry before becoming a full-time staff member at ZCLA. In my view, the incredible growth of the center during the late 1970s was primarily due to Tetsugen's leadership and energy. Of course, Maezumi Roshi supported his efforts, but he could

Tetsugen (Bernie Glassman) and Roshi, 1970

not have maintained such growth without Tetsugen.

At first I found Tetsugen as impenetrable as Mu. He was not very personable; but I came to realize that he just wanted everyone who sat with him to awaken to their Buddha Nature, and he felt at that time that intense, no-nonsense zazen was the way to do it. As the years went on, he softened, and I also opened up, and we became quite close. I now consider Bernie to be my closest Zen mentor.

○

In 1973, Marsha returned to the States from London. With the help of her parents, we bought a house in Encinitas, a small beach town in northern San Diego County. Although our marriage was doomed, it gave her a place to live with Sam and David while they grew up. Now, more than forty years later, Marsha is still living in that house. With Bill Henie's help, I was able to rent a small apartment in Encinitas that was on the cliff overlooking the ocean and Moonlight Beach. I spent as much time as I could with Sam and David, which was my joy as their father.

Also through Bill Henie, I met Sally Rorick, who became

a true love of mine. Sally was a single mother of a son who was Sam and David's age. She came from a well-established family in northern San Diego County. Sally had been raised Catholic and went to parochial school before graduating from Stanford University. She was a spiritual seeker who left the church and was looking for something different when we met. Sally began to meditate with me, and when Ray Jordan halted his weekly meditation meetings because of marital troubles, Sally and I started a weekly sitting group in my small Encinitas apartment. After a period of courtship, Sally and I moved together into the house next to my apartment on the Encinitas cliffs. Every morning we awoke to the sounds of the waves on the shore, and every evening we watched the sun sink into the ocean from our back patio.

Michael and Jan Soule, Joko on occasion, and a few others joined us for weekly zazen. One day Anne Saunders showed up. She was a bone fide hippy and a chemistry assistant at UCSD with a degree from Berkeley. She learned about our Zen meetings in a yoga class Sally ran. Anne Seisen became a regular Zen meditator and a good friend. Today she is a Zen teacher in National City, a town between San Diego and Tijuana, Mexico, having received Dharma transmission from Bernie.

Sally started attending sesshin at ZCLA with the rest of us. She immediately caught the eye of Dennis Genpo Merzel, who was a rising star. If memory serves, Genpo's first sesshin at ZCLA was also my first sesshin. He quickly moved to the Zen Center and was ordained as a monk with Maezumi Roshi. Genpo was very charming and personable, but he had many unlikable qualities as well. He became close to Maezumi Roshi and was one of his main drinking partners. Genpo and Bernie were close, as they were the most senior disciples, and spent much time with Maezumi Roshi planning the trajectory of

ZCLA and Zen in America. Genpo had an unhealthy attraction to women and hit on Sally and on every woman I brought to the center. Over the many years of our association, there were times when I admired what Genpo accomplished, and I often felt close to him, but I was never able to trust him, especially with women.

○

I continued to make my best effort in my practice, but I felt like a black lacquer bucket. In ancient times, a dull Zen student was called a black lacquer bucket because light would go in, but nothing would come out. When Maezumi Roshi would say that everyone had the wisdom and virtue of the Buddha, I was the one who would ask, "Can everyone realize their Buddha Nature?" since I was sure that I was the one exception. Roshi would say, "Sure, sure, sure!" He always had to pull me along.

At that time many students, including newcomers, would receive the Buddhist precepts in a ceremony called *jukai.* "Jukai" literally means "to receive the precepts," but Roshi said it means "to reveal yourself as the precepts." I did not take jukai because I did not feel that my practice was deep enough or that I was worthy. One day Roshi said, "You should take jukai." I said, "Will it help me pass through Mu?" Roshi said, "Sure, sure, sure!" So I decided to receive the precepts, become a Buddhist, and receive a Dharma name.

Roshi asked me a few questions to determine an appropriate name. I am a Leo, and my father gave me a Hebrew name, Tzadik Lev, which means Righteous Heart. Roshi decided to call me Shishin, which means Lion Heart. He also gave me another name, Ion. This Ion is not pronounced like the charged atoms in chemistry. The "I" is pronounced like the first syllable in Eeyore, the donkey friend of Winnie the Pooh, and the "on" is pronounced more like "own." So Ion is *ee-own*, which means "magnificent sound." The magnificent sound is the lion's inexhaustible roar.

Every day during sesshin we chanted the "Identity of Relative and Absolute," or *Sandokai* in Japanese. At the end of the chant is the line, "I respectfully say to those who wish to be enlightened, do not waste your time by night or day." I always tried to do my best and not allow my mind to wander. At first I read about holding your mind like a great iron wall against incoming thoughts. I became so attuned to incoming thoughts that I could feel a thought starting to form even before it appeared. It was like the earth bulging above a seedling before it breaks through the soil. This kind of practice was very exhausting. Later I learned to just allow my thoughts and feelings to arise but to subsume them in my breath and bring them into the ocean of my *hara,* the energy center in the lower abdomen that is the center of balance in our bodies. All rivers of thought flow to the ocean and become the one taste of the Dharma. I turned everything into the one taste of the ocean. In this way, my feminine side was emerging. The iron mountain was the masculine, samurai approach to zazen, and the

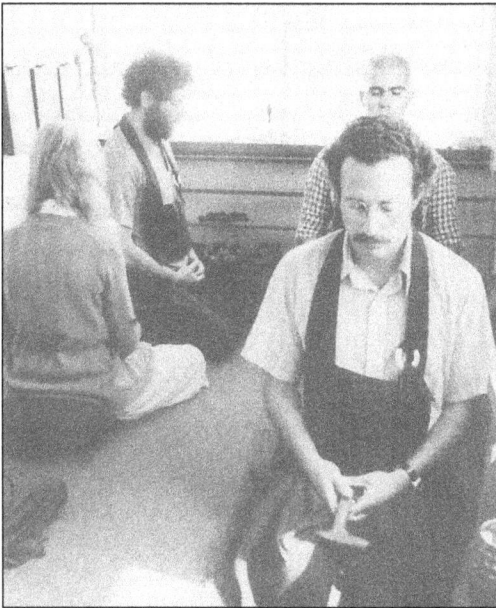

Here I am waiting for dokusan with Maezumi Roshi, 1974.

ocean was the receptive, feminine approach.

At ZCLA in the early days it was samurai all the way. During a weeklong sesshin in 1974, Maezumi Roshi and Bernie put a full-court press on me while I was working on Mu. During dokusan, Roshi would press me to show him Mu, and when I couldn't he would hit me with his stick (a short *kyosaku*) and ring me out of his room with his bell. Bernie would be waiting outside and send me back into the dokusan room, where Roshi would press me again. This went on a few more times until Bernie told me to sit down. I did. I sat down right in front of him on the floor in front of the dokusan room. My mind was no longer present. Bernie then directed this black lacquer bucket back to its seat in the zendo.

Around that time I had the most marvelous experience. While sitting during sesshin, I totally disappeared and only pure awareness remained. That awareness realized that it was a single-celled organism like an amoeba. Then it became a bigger blob like a jellyfish. Next it appeared as a fish and then a frog. It continued to manifest the evolutionary tree with birds, reptiles, mammals, and apes. Finally it was a human being with a kaleidoscope of shifting faces and shapes. The words of the Buddha resonated in my head: "I and all beings everywhere are simultaneously enlightened." I did not feel enlightened, but I definitely was simultaneously all beings everywhere. After that experience I looked at every one and every thing differently. I not only knew intellectually that we were connected, but I had no doubt that we are all one body.

○

After I had sat six years with Mu, three with Sochu and three with Maezumi, Maezumi Roshi must have sensed that I had buried myself deep in a rut with this koan, so he told

me to start working on a series of two hundred koans, which
we call the "Miscellaneous Koans," that are drawn from
a variety of koan collections. To my amazement, I had no
trouble penetrating these koans. Every time I met with Roshi
in dokusan I was able to correctly present a new koan. Seeing
the ease with which I presented these koans, Roshi said that I
must have seen something with Mu. Later I was able to pass the
"gateless gate" of Mu, but the early miscellaneous koans showed
me the way.

Examples of the "Miscellaneous Koans" are:
• How do you stop the sound of the distant temple bell?
• How do you stop suffering?
• Save a ghost.
• When the world was created, what was the creator like?
• Take a five-story pagoda out of a teapot.

You cannot unravel these koans through abstract thinking
with the conceptual mind. I spent the next eight years working
with Maezumi Roshi on the seven hundred koans that
comprise the curriculum in our lineage. It includes all of the
koans in the major collections: *The Gateless Gate, The Blue
Cliff Record, The Book of Equanimity, The Transmission of Light,
The Five Ranks of Tozan,* and one hundred koans about the
Zen precepts. My practice was like walking in a light mist and
suddenly realizing that I was soaked to the bone.

O

In 1977, Professor Isaacs arranged for me and Dave Castel,
an engineer from Israel, to take a piece of apparatus we had
developed to capture ocean wave energy and test it in the wave
climate of Hawaii. We spent three weeks in Honolulu and did
our experiments off Kaneohe Bay with support from the Naval
Research Center there and the University of Hawaii. During

Robert Aitken Roshi, 1978

our downtime, Dave sunbathed on Waikiki Beach and I went to the Diamond Sangha zendo to sit and study with Robert Aitken Roshi.

I knew Aitken Roshi from ZCLA. He was a successor of Koun Yamada Roshi and was the first American to be so recognized. Yet he felt too immature in his practice to assume the mantle of Roshi. So Aitken came to ZCLA for further study with Maezumi Roshi to firm up his understanding. Aitken Roshi spent considerable time at ZCLA, and we all got to know him through his presence and his talks.

I sat with the Diamond Sangha almost every morning before dawn. There, I met Nelson Foster, who assumed leadership of the sangha after Aitken died in 2010. One weekend, they had a *zazenkai*—all-day zazen with breaks only for meals. I continued my miscellaneous koan studies with Aitken Roshi, and we came up to a most difficult koan: "What is the source of Mu?" It is like another koan where a monk asked Joshu, "If everything returns to the one, what does the one return to?" Whatever you say cannot be the source since that arose from somewhere or from something.

Suddenly, the kid who had asked "Who created God?" when he was told that God created everything was faced with his own question. The Zen student has to exhaust all conceptual thought to penetrate this koan. Some students spend a year or more searching for this elusive source. Aitken Roshi rejected my first presentation, but he had no choice but to accept my second one as I had come up with the "classic" response. He told me to go on to the next koan.

When I returned to ZCLA, I asked Maezumi Roshi whether he wanted me to present the koans to him again. He said that he had talked to Aitken Roshi on the phone and that I should continue on. So, I thought to myself, these guys talk with one another about the intimate eye-to-eye exchanges that take place with students in the dokusan room! That was a revelation. At least I knew that Maezumi Roshi was keeping an eye on me.

I am indebted to Aitken Roshi for his willingness to share his training and understanding with me. For a long time, I remembered something he had said during a talk in Hawaii, and I cherished it. A few years later he appeared again at ZCLA and I told him how much I appreciated what he had said years before. And he said, "Oh, do you like that? I don't believe that anymore."

Everything changes. Aitken Roshi's little lesson was just the tip of the iceberg.

Chapter 6

Japan

> A monk asked Sozan, "When mourning
> clothes aren't worn, what then?" Sozan
> replied, "Today I have requited my filial
> piety." The monk asked, "After requiting
> filial piety, then what?" Sozan said, "I
> would love to get stumbling drunk."
> —*Book of Equanimity* Case 73

In 1975 Maezumi Roshi married Martha Ekyo. I missed the
wedding because I was in Japan. It was my first trip to Japan
and was courtesy of the Center for Marine Affairs at Scripps.
I was invited to give a presentation on ocean resources at the
Ocean Expo 75 that was taking place on the Japanese island
of Okinawa. I decided to parlay that trip into a two-week tour
of Japanese temples and monasteries and to visit several Zen
masters. I was very excited to be there. It was so exotic and
different from the Occident. At that time it was a challenge to
get around since no signs were in English and I did not read
any of the written forms of Japanese. I always had the names of
places I wanted to visit written down to show taxi drivers.

After the conference I flew to Tokyo where I was invited
to stay at Maezumi Roshi's family temple, Kirigayaji. Baian

Hakujun, Roshi's father, and his mother had seven sons. They all had the family name Kuroda, but to honor his mother, Roshi took her family name, which was Maezumi. There were no male heirs on the Maezumi family tree. All of the Kuroda sons but one became Zen priests. The youngest, Yoshikatsu, was a sculptor of religious objects.

Four of the brothers—Junyu, Motokyo, Kojun, and Yoshikatsu—were in Tokyo at the time I visited. I sat up drinking with them while Mrs. Kuroda, a very diminutive, energetic woman, scurried around serving everyone. The brothers and the mother were all friendly and interested in my relationship with Maezumi Roshi.

But when the father, Baian Hakujun, returned home, the atmosphere changed. It became imposing, impersonal, and demanding. Mrs. Kuroda fed him, drew his bath, gave him a massage, and served him a beer. He mostly ignored me. He did not have much of a grandfather mind. In contrast, Mrs. Kuroda thoroughly embodied grandmother mind.

Every morning I went to their shrine room to do zazen. They didn't ordinarily practice zazen. The temple was primarily set up for funerals and memorial services; the walls were lined with memorial plaques. I learned that Soto temples survive and thrive according to the devotion of their members in paying for memorial services for their ancestors. The spirit of zazen was dying. I cannot count the number of Zen Buddhists who told me that zazen was too hard and they were amazed that I was able to do it, especially since I was not Japanese. I can understand why Maezumi Roshi, Suzuki Roshi, and Sochu Roshi decided to teach Westerners. Generally speaking, we were more enthusiastic and serious, and they wanted to plant the Dharma seed on fertile soil where it would flourish.

Only Junyu would sit with me. He had been to ZCLA and

had trained everyone there in the zendo positions for our first ninety-day training period, or *ango*. He also asked one of his members who owned a taxi to schlep me to the most interesting sights in Tokyo.

While in Tokyo I went to Hannya Dojo—the place where Koryu Roshi lived and taught. Koryu Roshi was in the middle of a nine-hundred-day sesshin. Yes, *nine hundred* days—almost three years! Apparently he wanted to groom another successor or two. Every day Koryu Roshi sat six to eight hours and held dokusan two times. I was able to join them for an evening and a morning. I slept the night in a cramped dorm room with another student. Maezumi Roshi lived in Hannya Dojo while he was a student at the Komazawa Buddhist University. A young American student was living there during the nine-hundred-day sesshin, and we both realized later that he was Barry McMahon, who is now a Zen teacher in my lineage, the White Plum. After leaving Koryu Roshi, Barry became a jet fighter pilot in the U.S. Air Force, later studied with Maezumi Roshi, and eventually received Dharma transmission from Tenshin Fletcher, my Dharma brother.

Koryu Roshi was seventy-five years old when I visited, and he lived another ten years. I heard that he had been living in Nagasaki when the atomic bomb was dropped on that city. One of his eyes was cloudy and he wore thick glasses, but he seemed to have managed otherwise. I was most impressed that he was so steady in his commitment, even at his age. Koryu Roshi was a layman because his teacher, Joko Roshi, had been so disgusted by the corruption in the priesthood that he made Koryu vow to never become a monk. Koryu kept his promise and started a lineage of lay Rinzai teachers called Shakyamuni Kai. His motto was *"kai jo e,"* which means "precepts samadhi wisdom." As a layman, Koryu Roshi never minimized the importance

Koryu Roshi, 1974

of the precepts involving Right Action and Right Behavior, even though many Zen priests seemed to forget them. During the three-year sesshin, he was raising samadhi in those who participated, and he anticipated that wisdom would also arise in a few to carry on the Dharma.

Koryu Roshi wanted us to understand the relationship between our discipline (the precepts), our practice (samadhi), and realization (wisdom). We have all kinds of false understanding when we don't see clearly, when our vision is clouded. Not just in our practice, but in our everyday lives. Even today when we have satellite pictures from space, a "Flat Earth Society"—whose members believe the earth is flat— exists. Bigots still claim that the Holocaust did not happen, despite all the evidence to the contrary. What kind of vision do they have? It is easy to get confused if we don't have clear vision and see the root cause of things arising.

When winter approaches, the leaves fall from the trees and then it gets cold. If a person does not understand the root cause of the leaves falling, he or she might think that the leaves falling from the trees caused the weather to turn. I jokingly tell my students to scurry around to paste the leaves back on the trees to prevent winter from coming. If we don't see the true source, we run around confused, causing messes. It is easy to blame others for problems that arise in our lives. But if we look carefully, we see that we are the creators of our own attitudes. Ultimately there is no reason to complain about anything.

After the morning zazen, Koryu Roshi invited me to tea. Whereas I found Baian Hakujun to be cold and aloof, Koryu Roshi was engaging and warm. Maezumi Roshi was more like him than like his own father.

○

That afternoon Junyu put me on the train to Mishima, where Sochu Roshi's monastery Ryutakuji was located on the slopes of the picturesque Mount Fuji. Ryutakuji was founded by Hakuin Ekaku in the eighteenth century. Hakuin revitalized Rinzai Zen in Japan and prevented it from decaying. The koan system was becoming formulaic, and senior monks were selling koan answers to junior monks—a kind of Buddhist selling of indulgences. Hakuin reorganized and standardized the koan system and even created new koans, such as "What is the sound of one hand?" Modern pundits changed Hakuin's koan to "What is the sound of one hand clapping?" but that rendition is incorrect. There is no clapping for this one hand. I believe the word "clapping" was added to make the koan more approachable. I became intimate with Hakuin's one hand during my studies with Maezumi Roshi.

Hakuin was one of my favorites. He kept detailed journals about his spiritual journey that provided inspiration for those who followed. We learned about his struggles, triumphs, failures, arrogance, and fears. After attaining the state of no-doubt, Hakuin was a harsh critic of those who called themselves Zen teachers but had never had an awakening experience, or *kensho*. He said that their teaching is like leading people while sleep walking.

Sochu Roshi greeted me formally in his dokusan room and tested my Zen understanding. It was like old times. I wore my *rakusu*, a modified robe that looks like a bib and is given

Sochu Suzuki Roshi, 1970

to us when we receive the precepts. Sochu was most interested in the Dharma name I had received from Maezumi Roshi, which was written on the back of the rakusu. He read the name and told me that Shishin was going to sit alone with Hakuin. Every Zen temple and monastery has a founder's room with an altar containing remains of the founder plus a memorial plaque and a picture or statue. Sochu put me up in a guest room next to the founder's room. The guest room was a beautiful airy room filled wall-to-wall with tatami mats that opened to a Japanese garden with a pond, moss, and exotic plants—everything you could imagine seeing in a Japanese ink painting, or *sumi-e*. I slept on a futon that was stowed in a closet when I was not using it. Everything was efficient and orderly. I was in awe of the monks by the end of my stay.

Hakuin's founder's room felt dense and heavy in contrast to my room next door. At first I felt very uncomfortable sitting there alone with Hakuin. When he lived there, he would have his monks wrap a futon around him at night and tie him in while he sat in the zazen posture. He would sit like that all night long until they released him in the morning. Hakuin did not compromise and took no prisoners of those who wanted to study with him. Yet he also had his compassionate side.

There is a famous story of Hakuin involving a young woman in the village who became pregnant. When her parents pressed her, she lied and said the monk was the father. The parents approached Hakuin and told him that since he was responsible, he had to raise the child when it was born. All Hakuin said was, "Is that so." When the baby was born, Hakuin took him in and went on his traditional begging rounds carrying the child. As rumors spread, Hakuin had to go farther and farther away to beg for food since everyone started to avoid him. Finally the young women's guilt overcame her, and she confessed that her boyfriend had impregnated her, not the monk. The parents returned to Hakuin to take back the child and profusely apologized. Hakuin only said, "Is that so."

Each day, I sat on the cushion with Hakuin. I entered completely into my practice. I worked hard. I concentrated, but still felt stuck on something. I recalled Hakuin's writing about our self-grasping ignorance, which is the root of our delusive thoughts. What is that small line that keeps me anchored to the wharf? Hakuin said that the line is our attachment to the notion of "self." It is the root of our delusive thoughts. It's that instant of ignorance that has come down through endless eons of time. Our deluded image of reality arises because of its power. Although it's nothing but a chimera, it can stifle zazen more effectively than an army of ten thousand demons. When I examine carefully, it always comes down to this one belief: that the self is real, that "I" exists separate from everything else. That is self-grasping ignorance. No matter how hard I try, as long as I hold on to that belief, I will go nowhere. Thank you

Hakuin for reminding me where I am stuck. My final days with you were both intimate and profound.

O

I ate, bathed, and attended services with the monks. Every activity was a revelation. Since the monks were on a break between strict training periods, the meals were informal. We kneeled on the hardwood floor with a long bench in front of us. The cook brought the food and set it at one end. After chanting the meal prayer, we passed the food along the bench and served ourselves. It was usually miso soup, rice, and pickled vegetables. My legs had just about fallen off by the time we finished. How could those monks sit so long on their knees on a hard floor?

The baths were a different story. The monks started a wood fire under a big metal tub that had been filled with clean water. I was given a small cloth and told to use it to wash myself before getting in the tub. We crouched down, poured water over our heads from a bucket, soaped up, and rinsed. I had to rinse my cloth also since I learned that I was to use it to dry myself after the soak. But my mind complained. The cloth is damp; why don't you give me a dry towel like we do in my civilized country?

But despite my petty complaints, the baths were exquisite. All of the dust, aches, and pains were washed away. And then miraculously, the damp wash cloth dried my body. These monks knew what they are doing. I was completely refreshed and ready to join Hakuin once again.

At the end of the week, I bade farewell to Sochu Roshi. He walked me to the front gate where I was met by Yoshikatsu, who accompanied me on a sightseeing tour of Kyoto and Nara. That was the last time I saw Sochu. He died in 1990 in his mid-seventies.

○

Before leaving Japan, I made arrangements to visit Yamada Roshi in Kamakura. I arrived at the train station a few hours early and decided to see the Daibutsu, a famous statue of the Buddha that is so large it has a staircase inside for visitors to climb up and see through the eyes of the Buddha. Because of my nonexistent Japanese and poor directions from the locals, I spent two hours wandering around looking for the Daibutsu. When I found it, it was only two blocks from the train station. If you do not see the Way, you do not see it even as you walk on it.

Finally I was sitting with Koun Yamada Roshi, the man whose kensho experience as related in *The Three Pillars of Zen* had inspired me to start on the Zen path. Yamada Roshi was an administrator in a hospital and had a zendo behind his house. A significant proportion of his students were Americans and Europeans. Robert Aitken and scholar/teacher David Loy studied with Yamada and are two of the many people who became his successors in the Dharma. Yamada's long salt-and-pepper hair was slicked back, and while we sipped tea together, he brought out a huge cigar and started smoking. Not exactly how I pictured him. He was very kind and tried to nurture me through my koan study. I spent the night in his house before heading back to Tokyo and my long flight home.

When I saw Maezumi Roshi after my travels, he was interested in my encounters with the various Zen teachers. I asked him how I could repay their kindnesses. Roshi laughed and said, "Just sit well and they will be pleased." That is how to requite filial piety.

In the case presented in the epigraph to this chapter, Sozan says that he stopped wearing mourning clothes for his late teacher and had requited filial piety. How? Sozan had become completely independent. He essentially is saying, "I am complete as I am right now. What more needs to be done?" Could I say that I am independent? There's an easy way to find out. If there's anybody who gets under my skin, I am not independent. "Just sit well," and not only will my teachers be repaid and pleased, but I will be pleased as well. Then we can get stumbling drunk.

What kind of wine is Sozan talking about? Maezumi Roshi, who liked to drink, modified the Fifth Precept, which is often translated as "Abstain from taking intoxicating substances." Roshi said, "Do not drink the wine of delusion," or "Do not be ignorant." I found it interesting that a number of Zen teachers, not just Maezumi Roshi, changed the wording of the precepts so that they fit more with their personal lifestyles rather than being absolute commandments. So I say, "Let's drink the wine of freedom, independence, not being bound, the wine of appreciation of our lives and the lives of others." There is no intoxicating alcohol in that wine.

Chapter 7

Fork in the Road

When you come to a fork in the road,
take it.
—Yogi Berra

At the end of 1977 Sally and I had been living together for
a year on the cliffs overlooking the ocean in Encinitas. We
had a great relationship, and I had a great job on the beach at
the Scripps Institution of Oceanography. I was able to attend
sesshin every month with Maezumi Roshi, and we had a zazen
group that met in our little house. It was one of the happiest
and healthiest times of my life. So why was I restless?

In the thirteenth century Dogen completed his koan studies
in Japan with Myozen. Still harboring doubt, Dogen decided
to travel to China to find a more accomplished teacher. He told
Myozen that he wanted to go to the source and that if Myozen
was completely satisfied, he should stay, but if not, he should
accompany Dogen to China. Myozen went to China, too, where
he unfortunately died. But Dogen did find his true teacher and
after three years returned to Japan to become the most famous
Japanese Zen master of all time.

I had plenty of doubt about whether I was doing the best I
could with my life as an academic or whether I should devote

Sally Rorick in Hawaii, 1976

my life entirely to Zen. Joko had retired from the university and had moved to ZCLA a year earlier. Seisen and Myoyu had moved to ZCLA. A voice deep inside told me that I had to go there too. I asked Sally to go with me, but she had lived in Los Angeles and did not want to return there. A team of wild horses could not drag her away from her roots in northern San Diego County. And I realized that a team of wild horses could not keep me away from ZCLA. I sadly took my leave of Sally, Sam and David, and Professor Isaacs and headed north. Within a year, Michael Soule and Chozen and their three kids also joined us in the City of the Angels.

There was one complication. I had to have a job while living at the Zen Center to provide child support for Sam and David, who were seven years old. I looked around and was on the verge of getting a job teaching physics at a local LA university when Bernie told me that there was a place for me on the ZCLA staff and that the center would pay my child support. I jumped at it. I pictured myself weeding the garden in total peace when I wasn't sitting zazen. Wrong!

The first thing Bernie wanted me to do was head a fund-raising campaign for the center. I was to work with John Daido Loori, who had joined the ZCLA staff the previous year. Daido had met Maezumi Roshi, Bernie, and Genpo in Boulder where Trungpa Rinpoche had asked Maezumi to lead the seminary program at Naropa Institute while he was on solitary retreat.

Daido was on the summer staff of Naropa and was smitten by Maezumi Roshi. Bernie encouraged Daido to come to Los Angeles. Daido and I became quite close, and later when he was starting Zen Mountain Monastery, I helped him by leading programs and supporting his students.

ZCLA was exploding during the late 1970s. The zendo was filled to capacity for every sesshin, and we had to open a second zendo in one of the new buildings. Sometimes we even had a third meditation hall. To support the growth, Bernie encouraged people with skills to start businesses and give their earnings to the center. In time, we had Zen Landscaping, Zen Plumbing, Zen Carpentry, and Zen Painting. Chozen, who was a pediatrician, opened a Zen medical clinic, and Daido was the head of Center Publications, which published books on Zen practice, including a translation of Yamada Roshi's commentaries on the *Gateless Gate*. At its peak, the ZCLA staff numbered close to eighty.

Just as I was about to the join the staff, I participated in an ill-fated "friendly" softball game between ZCLA and Dharmadatu, a local Tibetan Buddhist group (now called Shambhala). While running around second base, I felt a snap in my right leg—my Achilles tendon had ruptured. I could not walk and had to have surgery to repair it. Fortunately I still had health insurance through the university, but unfortunately I had to wear a hard cast from my foot to my hip for three months. It put a cramp in my zazen, but somehow I figured out how to sit with the cast and did not miss a sitting. It took a long time for my leg to remember how to sit zazen after the cast was removed.

As soon as the cast came off, Maezumi Roshi told me that he wanted me to be ordained as a monk. Many of the staff were becoming monks, and once again Roshi was dragging me along. The capper was that he wanted me to be a celibate monk.

My *tokudo,* or Zen priest ordination ceremony, with Maezumi Roshi, 1978. Front row (*left to right*): Daido, Bernie Kakushin Silvers, and Genki.

I said that I was not interested; he told me in that case I could have a nice lay practice and did not have to be ordained. One or two monks were trying to be celibate, but there was no support for that kind of practice at ZCLA. Roshi was married. Bernie was married. Genpo was married but still had a roving eye. Lots of young men and women were jumping from one bed to another.

About two weeks later, Roshi changed his mind and told me that I could become ordained without being celibate. I assented and the date was set for December 1978. Even though Roshi paid lip service to lay practice, it did not hold the same value in his mind as practice as a monk or priest. All of his twelve successors became monks. I received monk's robes in the Soto style, a *kesa* (an outer robe that goes over one shoulder), a *zagu* (bowing cloth), and oryoki bowls. I had to relearn how to sit and how to bow while wearing my new habit.

No matter how hard I tried to have the robes look neat,

Roshi complained to me that I was not wearing them correctly. Much later, when I got new robes, I realized that my first set had not been my size. Don't blame me if they did not look right. I am not a shape shifter. Nonetheless, visiting Japanese priests must have thought that we looked like raggedy-ass cadets. They place a lot of stock on a monk's appearance as a reflection of his or her Zen mind.

◯

Daido and I ran a great fund-raising campaign. We got everyone involved and had training sessions on how to ask for money. One of our members, Stef Barragato, was a professional fund-raiser and gave us advice. Later, Stef became a successor of Bernie's before Stef's death in 2010. We raised $300,000, which our brochures said would be used for capital purchases to help the Zen Center expand. However, as the executive of ZCLA, Bernie did not allocate the money to those projects, spending it instead on other causes, which I am sure were also worthy. But after that experience, I have always been cautious with money around Bernie.

Bernie has raised a lot of money in his lifetime and taken some heat about his imputed lack of integrity about how he raised it and used it. In the more than forty years I have known Bernie, I have never seen him use money for his own personal luxury or comfort. He has always used money in the service of the Dharma, whether for the homeless, for the unemployed, for AIDS patients, for Buddhist scholars, for healing wounds of prejudice around the world, or for spreading his teachings of interconnectedness and the one body that includes all of us. He treated money like nutrients that he used to nourish those who were suffering.

After completing the fund-raising campaign, Bernie and

Roshi assigned me to help Michael Soule develop the Kuroda Institute for the Study of Buddhism and Human Values. Both Michael and I were academics, and the original idea was to create a college that focused on Buddhist education. Trungpa Rinpoche had founded the Naropa Institute (now Naropa University) in Boulder, Colorado, and we thought we could do something similar in California. Wrong again!

After much effort, we decided that our best choice, given our resources, was to create a think tank for Buddhist scholars. We recruited Buddhist scholars from around the country and planned to put on conferences to promote their work. We eventually formed an alliance with the University of Hawaii Press and ended up jointly publishing more than two dozen scholarly books on Buddhism. Peter Kakuzen Gregory, who was completing his Ph.D. in Buddhist Studies at Harvard, was our mainstay. He organized conferences, eventually took over leadership of the Kuroda Institute, and saw it through its halcyon years. After a successful academic career at the University of Illinois and at Smith College, Peter still holds the reins of the Kuroda Institute, which continues to co-publish books.

O

In 1976, Bernie had officially been named a Dharma successor of Maezumi Roshi, and in 1979 he left Los Angeles to move to his native New York to develop the Zen Community of New York. He was accompanied by Daido, their families, Paul Genki Kahn, and others. After humble beginnings, the Zen Community bought the Greyston mansion on the Hudson River through generous donations and loans. Bernie's showpiece, the Greyston Foundation, which became a model of nonprofit socially engaged corporations, was built up partially from the profits of the sale of the mansion.

Meanwhile, I continued to attend all of the zazen periods. We sat twice every day and had a weeklong sesshin every month. In 1979, Roshi selected me to be the head monk and to lead the ninety-day ango. During ango, we sat every day in the afternoon, in addition to morning and evening. The head monk is expected to attend all sittings, to lead chanting services three times every day, and to remain on the Zen Center grounds during the entire three-month period. During my tenure as head monk, Professor Isaacs died in San Diego. I was torn. My colleagues in San Diego urged me to honor him and attend his funeral service, but my duties as head monk forbade me from leaving the block. Once again, my idea of what it means to be a good Zen student won out. I had to honor Professor Isaacs by fulfilling my duties as head monk. I did not even ask Maezumi Roshi if I could go to San Diego, but I wish I had. That is one of many regrets in my life. Professor Isaacs was one of my dearest mentors.

New monk Shishin Osho, 1978

It was a long slog being present in the zendo for morning, noon, and evening service. During an ordinary service there are four main positions, the *ino,* or chant leader; the *doan,* or bell ringer; the person

who beats the mokugyo to keep cadence; and the officiant.
Often I was in the zendo alone and could only be the officiant,
especially on *hossan* days, the official rest days. On occasion,
residents would join me and take up positions. One women
I had been spending time with, Julie Doju Robbins, started
to show up every hossan day. She would be doan or beat the
mokugyo while I officiated, and we would chant together. I
very much appreciated her support. As I got to know her better,
I found that she is a most supportive person. Although we
came from quite different backgrounds, had different levels of
education, and at that time had divergent political views, and
in spite of a twelve-year difference in our ages, we started to get
closer and closer.

At the end of ango, the head monk gives a talk on a koan
case he or she had been studying with Maezumi Roshi and then
has to engage the assembly in Dharma combat to display his
or her understanding of the Dharma. I was very nervous since
some of ZCLA residents really liked to challenge you. I asked
Maezumi Roshi for advice and he said, "Don't think and just let
it come out." I remember little of that day other than looking
at the assembled students and telling myself that they were my
friends and wanted me to do well. I just let it come out.

○

Living at ZCLA still involved family for many of us. Sam
and David would take the coast commuter train from Del Mar
to Los Angeles Union Station, where I would pick them up
for weekends, usually twice a month. I would plan activities
on Sundays, which was our day off at ZCLA. Chozen had a
son, Noah, of the same age who would often hang out with
us. Julie's daughter, Janna, was two years younger, and all of
us would take in the latest Star Wars movie or some other

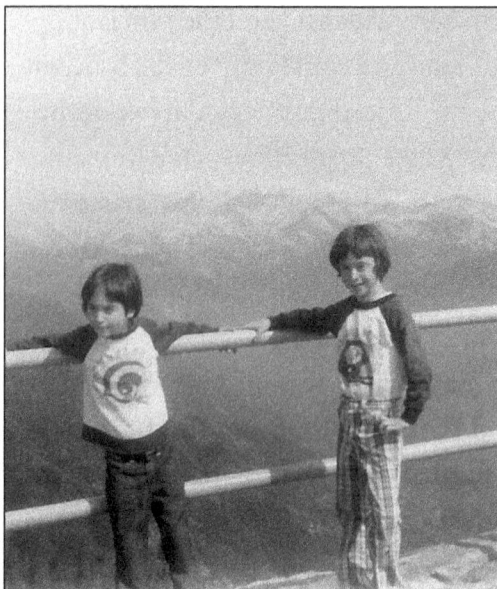

David and Sam on Moro Rock, 1980

blockbuster in Hollywood as a special treat. When the twins got older, they no longer wanted to leave their friends and take the train to LA, so I went to them.

All during my tenure with Maezumi Roshi, conflicts between family and duties as a monk kept arising. Roshi was married and had three children, but he was not a very devoted father or husband. In Japanese the word "monk" is translated as *unsui,* which means clouds and water. A monk flows without attachment like the clouds in the sky and the water in the river. The water in the streams never rests as it flows to the sea. When it enters the vast water, it becomes the endless waves. A monk leaves home and all worldly attachments. But not in Japan, and not in the United States. At first I thought Roshi would know how to deal with every situation because he was a Zen master. Wrong! I would never ask him how to raise my kids.

When I was living in Boulder, I heard the Dalai Lama give a talk. During the question-and-answer period, a woman asked him how to raise compassionate children. The Dalai Lama looked at her, laughed, and said, "How should I know? I am a monk." Even though he was a father, Maezumi Roshi did not know either.

Once when Sam and David were visiting, I got tickets to
a USC football game that was at the LA Coliseum a few miles
from the Zen Center. Less than a hour before we were to leave
for the game, Roshi summoned me to accompany him for
a meeting with Bishop Yamashita, the head of the Soto Zen
mission in the United States, located in the Little Tokyo district
of Los Angeles. I had to scurry around to find someone to take
the boys to the game. Paul Chigen Jaffe volunteered and they
had a good time, but I was miserable sitting quietly and missing
being with my boys while Roshi and the bishop conversed in
Japanese. This was a theme that came to a head between me
and Roshi.

$$\Omega$$

I started to assume more teaching responsibilities after my
stint as head monk. I began leading the Introduction to Zen
classes on the weekends and mentoring newcomers to the Zen
Center. Roshi would often take me with him when he led out-
of-town sesshin. We went to Northern California to conduct
session at the home of Arvis Justi, who introduced Adyashanti,
a popular teacher, to Zen. I went to Arizona to lead sesshin,
and Roshi also sent me to Mexico City to establish a Zen center
there. Mexican pilgrims had been coming to Los Angeles in
ever increasing numbers, and the time was ripe for ZCLA to
have a presence in Mexico—and I was it.

At first I accompanied Maezumi Roshi to Mexico City to
assist him with sesshin. Then I started to go by myself and
set up a more permanent center, Centro Zen de México, first
in the Coyoacan district and then in San Angel. I started
staying for two and three months at a time. Over a period of
about three years I spent about a third of my time there. The
Mexican students were passionate and devoted, and the center

Me leading *kinhin* (walking meditation) in Mexico, 1983

gradually started to grow. However, the same class tensions that occurred in Mexican society started to occur in our little sangha. As an outsider I did not appreciate the hidden feelings between the über rich and the middle class. Some members of our sangha were quite wealthy, including those from leading manufacturing families and high-ranking political families, as well as doctors, lawyers, and academics. We also had working-class members, some of whom complained to me in private about their treatment from the gentry. When I talked to one of the privileged women about it, she said, "Well, we don't wear our jewelry in the zendo, do we?"

I was able to hold the disparate groups together as I gave them a lot of slack. After I left, the sangha split along class lines, and then the upper-class sangha split along gender lines. One of my aims was to encourage the upper-class members, who were attended by many servants at home, to pay attention to the effects of their actions. During sesshin, participants would smoke outside the building and then throw their butts on the ground. During *samu,* or work practice, I would have them clean up their butts and sweep the grounds. During the next break they were out there again, smoking and discarding their butts on the ground. And they had to clean it up again during samu. When they finally learned to properly discard their butts, I had them clean the streets and common areas in front of the building. I told them that Mexico City would become shiny because of their efforts. I told them, "Poco a poco, se va lejos"—little by little, one goes a long way.

One of the members, Rudolfo Agarrio, was on the national commission for the preservation of the monarch butterfly. Monarchs migrate thousands of miles between Colorado and Mexico, where they cluster on the oyamel trees that grow only in limited mountainous areas. On one occasion when Maezumi Roshi and Julie were in Mexico, Rudolfo made arrangements for us to visit the monarch sanctuary near Mexico City and was

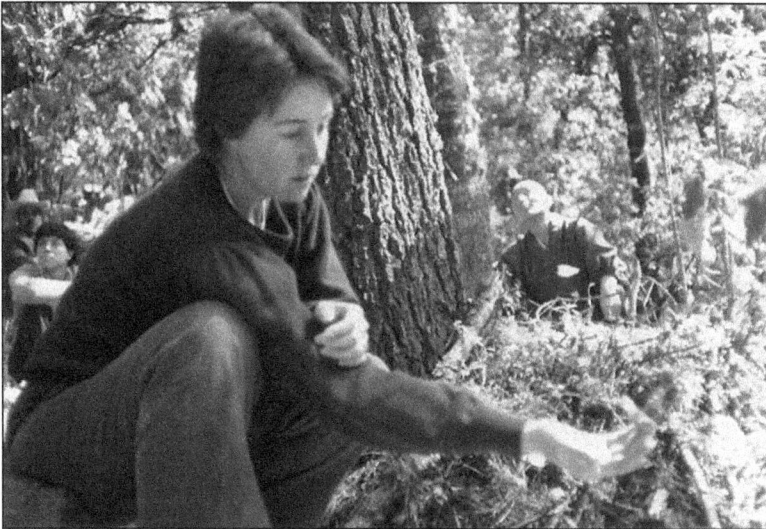

Julie and Roshi interacting with monarch butterflies in Mexico, 1983

able to pinpoint their location. We had to trek up and down steep ravines at high altitude. Rudolfo and I had to assist Roshi and Julie, but it was worth the effort. Thousands of clusters of thousands of butterflies draped from the trees. It was like a magical, enchanted land. Mother Nature is truly amazing.

On another occasion we held a sesshin in an empty house that had just been completed by Niso Bejar, an architect who sat with Centro Zen de México. During sesshin, the neighbor's dog ran out in the street and was killed by a car. Maezumi Roshi told me that we were responsible. I asked, "How are we responsible?" assuming that I would hear a Zen teaching on how we create our own reality and are responsible for it. But instead he said, "This house was empty, and then suddenly we are thirty people walking around, ringing bells, and chanting. The dog got disoriented and ran into the road. We have to give him a proper funeral service." One of our members went to the neighbor and proposed the funeral, and somewhat to my surprise, the neighbor readily accepted. We dug a hole in the garden and carried the dead dog in a full procession with

Roshi facing practitioners at Centro Zen de México sesshin, 1983

robes, bells, incense, and chanting. Then we ceremoniously laid the dog to rest and prayed that he would have a rebirth in more fortuitous circumstances. The neighbor was most grateful and wished us a speedy journey to nirvana. We can never know all the conditions that affect our lives and our decisions. But one thing I do know: we are responsible.

Chapter 8

Upheaval

Without the bitterest cold that penetrates
to the very bone, how would plum
blossoms send forth their fragrance all
over the universe?
—Dogen in *Eihei Koroku*

Julie Doju Robbins and I decided to get married in 1982
and share our lives together supporting the Dharma. Maezumi
Roshi performed the ceremony at ZCLA in February, and Joko
and Michael Soule stood with us. Our children, my mother,
and my brother Alan were also present and offered encouraging
words. Mother loved to visit the Zen Center because the people
were so kind and respectful toward her. Since she was Jewish
to the core, she never made the connection that their actions
might have something to do with their Buddhist practice.

My mother had been widowed for thirteen years at that
time. She never had an interest in meeting a new man and
desperately clung to her children. When I was growing up,
I found her to be suffocating and tried to keep my distance.
A ZCLA member, Harry Brickman, who was a successful
psychiatrist and UCLA professor, once told me, "The more I sit,
the better I listen to my patients, the less I have to say to them,

Julie's and my wedding ceremony with Maezumi Roshi, 1982

and the better they get." After years of zazen I found that I was able to spend time in my mother's presence without tuning her out. I started to listen to her and hear what she was saying. This listening had the overall effect of calming her down. We learned to be lovingly present with each other without negative reactions on either side. I am happy to say that through the power of zazen, I made peace with my mother before she died in 1989.

$$\bigcirc$$

With the departure of Bernie, Genpo became the executive director of ZCLA. He lacked the mental and intellectual acuity of Bernie but used his charm and warm personality to keep the center solvent and sustainable. I still was traveling to Mexico regularly, and when I was on the ZCLA campus, I was Genpo's assistant and helped to oversee all of the center's operations.

One smart thing I did was put the center's records on computers. Even with ZCLA's growth, all of the finances and membership records were still kept by hand. So with the price of personal computers coming down, we decided to computerize everything. Larry Jissan Christensen and I did the legwork identifying the system for our needs, and then Rick Doshin Sailor and I did all of the programming. I had learned to program in college, and Rick was a computer science graduate. I had to learn BASIC for the system we bought, and with Rick's guidance, we were able to simplify the tedious way ZCLA kept its information.

Since I enjoyed programming so much, I scrimped to buy a small Atari computer and wrote educational programs for my kids that were published in popular computing magazines. I even attended night school at UCLA to learn the latest C programming language, and I joined a local computer club to learn more. I mention all of this because it stood me in good stead when I left ZCLA and reentered the workforce to support my growing family.

Julie became pregnant at the end of 1983. It was a fertile time at the Zen Center; at least three other women were pregnant at the same time. Julie had previously had a miscarriage, so when her contractions started at the beginning of her eighth month, we became concerned and went to the hospital. The doctors and nurses did what they could to calm the contractions, but they did not have the right tools in their tool chest. They decided to give Julie steroids to help develop the baby's lungs to increase his chances of survival since they thought his birth was imminent. But then my Zen kicked in. I told Julie to chant the "Enmei Jukku Kannon Gyo" with me—the short Japanese chant that invokes Kannon, the Bodhisattva of Compassion. We started to chant, and the nurses and doctors looked at us with interest and skepticism. They held off on the steroids as we chanted for thirty minutes, then an hour. The contractions quieted down and eventually stopped after two hours of chanting. There was no longer any need for steroids.

Later, a nurse discovered that hospital staff had misread a test and Julie in fact had a urinary tract infection that caused the contractions. Some antibiotics cleared that up, and she delivered a healthy boy at full term on August 2, 1984. We named him Daniel James Wick.

Now I never underestimate the power of prayer, chanting, and invoking holy names. I started to view our chanting services at the Zen Center with new eyes. Every time I chant, I send good merit to those around the world who suffer and need comfort. When I travel by plane, I chant during takeoffs and landings and send the merit to the pilots and all of the working parts of the airplane. So far it has worked. And if the Bodhisattva someday does not heed my incantations, at least I will die chanting. What better way to go?

O

Doing zazen in the middle of a dirty, noisy, crowded city such as Los Angeles is a challenge for many people. At times during sesshin we would hear a loud crash as cars outside collided. Nobody would get up to check, but everyone was thinking, "I hope that wasn't my car parked on the street that got crunched." Sitting with a police helicopter clattering overhead was like sitting on a factory floor. And then there were the earthquakes. If you think you have transcended life and death, try sitting through an earthquake in a sixty-year-old building that has a weak foundation.

It is not surprising that there was a movement to

Procession at Zen Mountain Center, 1986. *Left to right:* Tesshin, Jitsudo, me (with hair), Roshi, Tenshin.

relocate ZCLA to the country where the air was fresh and the atmosphere was quiet. By chance, one of our members, Tom Fresh, and his girlfriend Lucinda owned 160 acres near the town of Idyllwild in the mountains two hours east of Los Angeles. Tom was willing to deed the land to ZCLA in exchange for our paying the mortgage and allowing him to live out his life there. We consummated the deal in 1982, and Zen Mountain Center was born (now called Yokoji-Zen Mountain Center). At first we erected army tents to host sesshin. Then through the efforts of Tenshin Fletcher and Jitsudo Ancheta, a few buildings went up. When Jitsudo left to go to New Mexico, Tenshin and Seisen took over the management of the Mountain Center and grew it to the next level. When Seisen left to go to San Diego, Tenshin continued the construction and has developed it into one of the most beautiful and compelling Zen training centers in North America.

I remember sitting many sesshin there and smiling when the noisy squirrels started chittering and blue jays started

98

screeching. The distraction was not too different from the squealing of car tires in the city. When the wind picked up, large pine cones dropped on the zendo roof with a big thud that would have woken Rip Van Winkle. Then there were the rains and the erosion caused by flash floods. At times in the winter, snow prevented cars from driving the mountain road into and out of the Mountain Center. When people complained about sitting in the city, I would recall a "Far Side" cartoon of two bears wearing trench coats and hats walking down a busy city street. One says to the other, "It always takes me a few days to unwind after I come down from the woods." If you cannot sit in the city, you probably cannot sit in the country either.

Upon being enlightened by the sound of a rushing stream, Shisen, an ancient Zen master, wrote, "The stream's rippling is the eloquent tongue of the Buddha, and the mountain's contour is the body of the Buddha." Why not "the cacophony of city traffic is the eloquent tongue of the Buddha, and the stinking pile of trash is the body of the Buddha"? Buddha Nature appears in the city, in the wilderness, in a grain of sand, and in vast space.

○

Maezumi Roshi liked to do things by the book—that is, the Soto playbook. It was time for Bernie to "ascend the mountain" and become abbot of the Zen Community of New York. I imagine since most ancient monasteries were located in remote mountains, the abbotship ceremony assumed such a name. An elaborate ceremony and celebration were planned to take place at Greyston mansion. Roshi took me there as his personal attendant, and I was part of the procession accompanying Bernie to his mountain seat. Hundreds of people were invited, including prominent Buddhist teachers from around the country.

We arrived a few days early to help with preparations. Every morning we had zazen and Roshi conducted dokusan for the residents of the Greyston mansion. Part of my duty was to ring the bell signaling the beginning and end of dokusan. The last person meeting with Roshi had spent more than thirty minutes with him. Preparations were being made for lunch, and there was lots of commotion around me, so I decided that I did not have to ring the concluding dokusan bell and put it away. When Roshi rang his bell signifying that he was done, Bernie showed up from nowhere and said, "Did you ring the concluding dokusan bell?" I was already at the lunch table and had to run back to fetch the bell and ring it. Another Zen teaching moment. I had created a tear in the space/time continuum.

Bernie always puts on a good show. During part of the ceremony he engaged the assembly in Dharma combat. With ease and humor, Bernie dispatched all challengers. I could really see the value of his training with Maezumi Roshi and

Bernie Tetsugen and Roshi greeting after Mountain Ascension Ceremony, 1982

the results of his own hard effort.

But Bernie took shortcuts too. The buildings ZCLA owned had been modified to accommodate the meditation halls, kitchen, common spaces, and offices. It all had been done without building permits, as is still common for most small Buddhist centers. After the center had been there for almost twenty years, the city got wind of us and we were suddenly in their spotlight. It was my job to meet with our city councilman and his staff and make arrangements to get a zoning variance so we could conduct our affairs legally.

The first things I did were to arrange for Councilman Cunningham to have lunch with me, Roshi, and Genpo and then to address our community. I also contacted every Buddhist group in Los Angeles and invited them to come to ZCLA to hear the councilman speak. There was (and is) a Vietnamese Zen temple just down the street from ZCLA. Kwan Um Sah had a Korean Zen temple in the neighborhood,

Me, Roshi, and Genpo with Councilman Cunningham, 1982

and a Tibetan Buddhist group was also not far away. On the appointed day more than 250 people gathered in ZCLA's backyard to face the councilman. I knew that he counted votes, and after the gathering, our variance went through the city without a hitch.

When I was in college, I had a summer job as a janitor at Disneyland. Every day there was a parade of exotic animals down Main Street. One of the janitors had to push a cart and shovel up all the poop dropped by the elephants, camels, llamas, horses, and other quadrupeds. We called that cart the honey bucket. At ZCLA I felt like I was constantly pushing the honey bucket, cleaning up messes that those who came before me had made.

However, my honey bucket was not big enough to contain all of the shit that next hit the fan. At a staff meeting in 1983 Maezumi Roshi admitted that he had been sleeping with several students, including Chozen, his Dharma successor. The idol fell hard off his pedestal. In the community I could see the five stages of grief and loss—denial, anger, bargaining, depression, and finally acceptance—being played out simultaneously.

Some people denied it; others were angry—some at Roshi, others at Chozen. Some were full of alternate scenarios: if only we had done this, then that would not have happened. Others got depressed, and very few, mostly the non-Americans, were able to accept the situation. I was primarily sad but also angry. When my confusion subsided, I knew that I had to do whatever I could to help.

Chozen became a scapegoat, which was unfortunate but easy to understand. Many students did not want to blame Roshi since he was supposed to be the perfect master, so Chozen was an easy mark. Chozen had been my friend for many years; we had spent a lot of time together in San Diego. Shortly after she had come to the Zen Center, she had an affair with Genpo. She ended that and started hanging out with Bernie and his family. Then she started spending all her time cloistered with Roshi working on "important Dharma matters." I know that she cared about others, but I felt that she projected an attitude of superiority that alienated people, including me. Roshi did not help matters by telling his other female students that they should be more like Chozen.

It was clear by that time that alcohol was a major contributor to the problems. The senior students intervened and urged Roshi to go to an alcoholic rehabilitation center. Bernie had left. Genpo had been going to Europe to establish the White Plum lineage there and was about to leave. Chozen was compromised. Joko had returned to San Diego and established the Zen Center of San Diego. I was the next most senior student and had to take a major role in healing a badly wounded community.

Roshi entered the Betty Ford Center. His attendant, Bill Yoshin Jordan, was most instrumental in getting him there and helping clean up the damage. We had many community meetings with outside facilitators who were alcohol dependency counselors, community workers, and psychotherapists. Most of the meetings were heated. People felt betrayed by Roshi and by Chozen, and they threw Genpo in the mix because he had also abused his leadership position by sleeping with many of the women at ZCLA.

Disillusioned members left in droves. When the dust settled, the staff had dwindled to four people: I was the administrator, Myoyu was the treasurer, Seisen was the program director, and Marsha Fumyo Jensen was the secretary. As often happens in similar situations, a shadow sangha formed. People who wanted nothing more to do with ZCLA continued their friendships outside the center and often sat together and complained about how they had been betrayed.

As part of his rehabilitation, Roshi had to meet with the people closest to him in an open-hearted, honest session. Those who participated included his wife, Ekyo; his oldest daughter, Michi; and Genpo, Chozen, Yoshin, and me. As part of the exercise, Roshi had to sit face-to-face with each of us in turn and express how he felt about us. It was obviously hard for him. He did not know his own feelings unless the discussion came to how people were progressing on the traditional Zen path.

When it was my turn, Roshi said that he did not like how I

First meeting of Soto Zen bishops in LA, October 1981, at Zenshiji, the main Soto temple in the Little Tokyo district. First row (*left to right*): Bishop Gyokuei Matsuura of Hawaii; Maezumi Roshi; Rev. Shinkai Miyamoto, director of the educational division of Japanese Soto headquarters in Japan; Bishop Ryohan Shingu of South America; Bishop Yamashita of North America; and Bishop Deshimaru of Europe. Second row (*left to right*): Shizan Watanabe (a young Rinzai monk who lived at ZCLA for a few years), Bernie Kakushin Silvers, and two students of and translators for Deshimaru Roshi. Third row (*left to right*): Dosho Saikawa (a young Soto monk who lived many years at ZCLA and later became bishop of South America), Adele Myoku Silvers, Joko, me, and Genpo.

had not been in the zendo one night when he was entertaining a Japanese priest. I had been living at ZCLA for six years by then. I never missed a sitting unless there was an emergency. One night I decided that Julie and I needed a treat, so we went to play tennis with Genro Gauntt and his wife, Laura Barbara. On the way back, while I was wearing my tennis shorts and carrying a tennis racquet, Roshi turned the corner with his Japanese dignitary, and there we were, facing each other. If that was the worst he thought of me, I felt most fortunate!

When he returned to ZCLA Roshi was very contrite and continually apologized for causing disharmony in the sangha. If it had not been for that, I might not have stayed. I know that I would not have abandoned my father if he were an alcoholic and tried to correct his ways. Causing disharmony in the sangha is one of Buddhism's five gravest sins. The other four are killing your father, killing your mother, killing an *arhat* (an enlightened being), or causing bodily injury to the Buddha. Those who commit even one of these sins are immediately reborn in Hell. We lived in the hellish realms at ZCLA for many years. It was not until twenty years later through the efforts of Wendy Egyoku Nakao as ZCLA abbot that the oppressive atmosphere lifted.

Before entering the Betty Ford Center, Roshi had given Dharma transmission to Genpo, Joko, and Chozen. I had just finished koan practice. He wanted to give me Dharma transmission when he returned from treatment, but I told him no. The atmosphere at the Zen Center was very depressed, and it did not feel appropriate for me to receive transmission in that environment. It was another four years before Roshi persuaded me to do it.

Genpo left for Europe where he established a very strong practice, but he continued over the years to get in trouble with his abuse of power. Chozen and Michael divorced, and she left for Oregon where she started the Zen Community of Oregon with Laren Hogen Bays and eventually founded the Great Vow Monastery. Since she suffered so much, Chozen became a persistent campaigner for clear ethical guidelines for Zen teachers in the United States. Some people questioned the validity of her empowerment since she had slept with her teacher. I think she was relieved when I told her that I had never questioned her understanding of the Dharma. Joko cut off completely with Maezumi Roshi. I tried to get them together, but Joko always refused. She said that Roshi was stuck in his Japanese ways, lacked emotional insight, and would never "get it." She never made an effort to reconcile.

Roshi was very subdued for a long time. In our private moments, he sometimes ranted about how puritanical Americans are; and then he would say that what he did was inexcusable, especially sleeping with Chozen, a Dharma successor. He continued to drink, but never in public—just in the privacy of his own room. He never made excuses and never stopped apologizing.

I see our cultural conditioning as a part of the problem. Roshi was Japanese, and he never adapted to American ways. In Japan, they don't call a person who drinks excessively an alcoholic; instead, they say, "He likes sake." And women are demeaned in Japan. Japanese men, and Zen priests are no exception, treat women as inferior objects. I believe that it is nearly impossible for anyone to transcend his or her cultural conditioning. Almost all Japanese Zen teachers who came to this country in the middle of the last century were alcoholics or sexual predators or both. In the recent high-profile cases of sexual predation by Eido Shimano and Joshu Sasaki, they never apologized for their actions. I was relieved that Maezumi Roshi did.

Still, I have been asked many times why I continued to support Maezumi Roshi. For an answer, I created this story. If I wanted to study the violin, I would find the best violin teacher I could. If that teacher drank or was mean to her children, it would not diminish my teacher-student relationship as long as I got the best musical instruction possible. Maezumi Roshi was the best Zen teacher available to me. I cannot repay him for all I learned from him. I was greedy for the Dharma, and he was a genuine vessel. But you ask, shouldn't Zen understanding apply to one's whole life? What kind of teachings are Zen teachers transmitting if they continue to be handicapped by their addictions and shortcomings? Is it possible to receive life-changing teachings from "imperfect" teachers? I think it is. We always have to use our discerning wisdom to separate the wheat from the chaff.

Hakuin said that practice after *satori,* or a deep enlightenment experience, is more difficult than practice before satori because of our "habit-ridden consciousness." Our habits include all of our conditioning and beliefs that are either hidden or not questioned. Even in the Declaration of Independence it says, "We hold these truths to be self-evident . . ." Self-evident truths are our habit-ridden consciousness. In Zen there are no self-evident truths. Every truth has to emerge from the ground of not-knowing. As the Zen poem *Hsin-Hsin Ming* says: Do not seek for the truth; just cease to cherish your opinions.

Roshi decided that he and I should study the precepts together. I had already gone through the one hundred koans based on the precepts with him, but he wanted to do it again. This time we went to another level; he did not accept facile answers. The precepts are not a set of strict commandments. There are many nuances, and that is how it is possible to get into trouble.

For example, the precept of non-killing says, "Honor life. Do not kill." From a literal standpoint, it means do not take any life. Do not take the life of anything. But we have to eat living beings in order to survive. Isn't that killing? And what about time? If we waste time, we are killing it. What about space? Or inanimate objects such as tiles or needles or tools? The literal interpretation does not always apply. Everything depends upon conditions, and there might be a time when taking life is appropriate. Suppose a rabid dog is attacking your child. What would you do?

The interpretation that can cause the most problems is the "emptiness" interpretation. Since ultimately the self does not exist and others do not exist, who is killing whom? In this scenario there is no separation, and even killing does not exist. In my opinion it takes a totally enlightened being to implement this interpretation, and I have to admit that I have never met one.

There are shadow sides to all the interpretations of the precepts. If one sees this world of emptiness and sticks to it, that insight can become dangerous. Pure wisdom, or deep insight, can be dangerous when it is not accompanied by compassionate action that is based on the oneness and interconnectedness of all beings. Those Zen teachers who emphasize the emptiness interpretation of the precepts without embracing the literal and conditional interpretations are the ones who cause the most damage to the Dharma and the Sangha. Those who stick to the literal view become rigid and inflexible and tend to lack heart. The conditional view can lead to confusion about the best action to take. All three taken together are needed to lead a compassionate life.

〇

Julie and I had been discussing leaving ZCLA and returning to San Diego. Dan was one year old and we did not want to raise him in the rough neighborhood where the center was located. Also, Sam and David were entering adolescence and needed to have their father nearby.

When things started to quiet down, the vitality of the Zen Center was gone. Half of the people had left. We could not sustain all of the buildings and grounds and programs. We had to cut back, and I felt that it was on my shoulders to keep the ship from sinking. I knew what needed to be done, and I told Roshi that I would do it. I would stay for one more year, but then I would leave.

Chapter 9

Back to Lay Life

> Spirit-like understanding and divine
> functioning lie in carrying water and
> chopping wood.
> —Layman P'ang

Three major problems needed to be addressed at ZCLA in 1984. The first was the financial situation. We were bleeding money. Since the participation in programs and membership had dropped so much, we could not pay our operating expenses. The second was a lawsuit against the Zen Center by Bernie Kakushin Silvers, who felt that the center and its officers, including Roshi, Bernie (Tetsugen), Genpo, and me, had not fulfilled our obligations to him. He was particularly concerned about a house that he had donated to the center, but it seemed to me that he had donated the house with the expectation that in return the center would provide for him and his new family. The third was the medical clinic that Chozen had started. She had brought a doctor, Debbie Satterfield, into her practice and had left without any clear plans for the future of the clinic.

Grover Genro Gauntt, a ZCLA board member and long-time student of Roshi's, helped me solve the problems. He had a real estate appraisal business that he ran out of the Zen Center, and in consultation with the rest of the board and Roshi, we decided that we needed to sell the buildings on the lower half of the block, which included two apartment buildings and three houses. The buildings were eventually sold to a Korean developer, and the finances were in order for years to come. After earning his living in real estate for many years, Genro has become a major advocate of homeless street retreats around the world. Participants in street retreats take a plunge into the unknown where they live on the streets of a large city with no money. They have to bear witness to being and figure how to survive as a homeless person. As a group, the participants regularly meet in a public park to meditate together and to reflect upon their experiences. Bernie started the street retreats, and Genro studied with him and received Dharma transmission from him.

The lawsuit was trickier. Bernie Silvers had been the center's attorney, and now he was suing us. Roshi, Genro, and I started interviewing attorneys to represent ZCLA. We selected Hal Stanton, who was a high school friend of mine. Hal and I had reconnected when he used ZCLA's landscaping business, Zen Landscaping, to do some work at his home in the San Fernando Valley. He had collected Zen art for years and just started a meditation practice. After the lawsuit was concluded, he became a legal advisor to the Zen Center.

The tricky part of the lawsuit was that Bernie Silvers and Bernie Glassman are first cousins. The two of them had verbally made all the property agreements and nothing had been recorded. Bernie Glassman was in New York, and we eventually had to fly him to Los Angeles when we had the first court hearing. Bernie Silvers had made a motion to the court to halt the sale of the Zen Center property to the

Korean developer to force us to settle with him. The judge ruled in favor of ZCLA. After that ruling, the two Bernies sat down and worked out an agreement that Hal Stanton, Roshi, Genro, and I could accept. We ended up giving Bernie Silvers a financial settlement in exchange for his dropping all claims against the center.

With the medical clinic, there were issues of patients' records, insurance, and ownership. Debbie wanted to maintain the clinic, but she had to move because we were selling the building that housed her office. There were also outstanding bills that we had to negotiate. After months of going back and forth, we resolved all of the problems, and Debbie claimed ownership of the clinic and relocated to another neighborhood.

I had fulfilled my promise to Roshi that I would relieve all of ZCLA's major headaches. Now I could prepare to leave. But there was one major hurdle that I had to clear. I had no money. When I joined the staff I received $50 per month plus room and board. When I ordained, I took a vow of poverty. Anything extra had to come from the savings I had when I joined the staff. After almost eight years, my savings were gone. When Julie left the ZCLA staff she found work as a legal secretary in downtown LA and was able to cover some of our expenses. The ZCLA board offered to provide me with a severance stipend of $500 per month while I reestablished myself in the workforce. But that was not enough to get us started. Fortunately, Julie had saved several thousand dollars from her salary. Without her money, we could not have made it.

Michael Soule had returned to San Diego and offered Julie, Dan, and me a room in his house. Without his kind assistance, life would have been much tougher. Since I was Roshi's senior student in Southern California, Roshi wanted me to continue to assist him with sesshin, rituals, ceremonies, and other official Zen activities. For the next ten years I retraced my steps either to ZCLA or to the Mountain Center near Idyllwild to give Dharma talks and see students in private interviews as an assistant teacher.

As one sesshin was nearing its end, I had finished all of my duties. No more students wanted to see me, so I decided to leave a few hours early and go back to San Diego to spend time with Dan and Julie before Monday when I continued my job search. Roshi complained to someone about my lack of commitment, and word got back to me. I was furious. I wrote him a letter and told him that here in America we talk directly to people when we have an issue with them. In Japan, one always goes through intermediaries, and over the years when Roshi had a complaint about Genpo, for example, he would tell Bernie or me rather than speak directly to Genpo. I wrote Roshi that I wanted him to talk to *me* if he had a complaint about me. And I said that I would no longer accept the severance allowance from ZCLA, even though I could not survive without it. When he received the letter, Roshi immediately called me and apologized. From that time forward, he was always gracious with me and grateful for whatever help I gave him. He even tried to talk directly with me when issues arose.

I had managed to pick up a contract programming job to keep food on the table until something more permanent came along. Finally I was offered a job writing software for a company, Action Instruments, that built controllers for factory automation and control. It was a stretch for me. I took more night classes at UCSD in UNIX programming and devoured computer handbooks and manuals. If a computer game or a word processor crashed, there would be no catastrophic consequences. But now I had nagging thoughts about molten iron spilling on a factory floor because of an error in my software code. Luckily it never happened.

The president of Action Instruments was a man from India name Jim Pinto. He and his lieutenants were members of the Toastmasters Club, which promotes public speaking as a means of gaining self-confidence. On the weekends, Pinto required certain employees to meet and prepare presentations for each other. He even gave cash prizes. Since I had spent several years giving Dharma talks at ZCLA and leading meetings, it was not stressful for me to talk in front of a bunch of engineers, accountants, and salespeople. They particularly loved my talk about how Action Instruments was like a Zen monastery. I kept winning the cash prizes until I was no longer required to participate. But I did catch Pinto's eye, and he kept promoting me to positions of more responsibility. I was able to hire Rick Sailor to join my group, and his software savvy rescued our projects on numerous occasions. Rick eventually left Action Instruments and went to Microsoft, where he made a small fortune.

Over the next few years I led workshops on "Zen in the Workplace" at the Mountain Center and published an article in *Tricycle* magazine on the same topic. At these workshops I often quoted the Zen expression, "When the country prospers, the king's name is unknown." Only when there are problems does everyone know who to blame. Of course, like all Zen expressions, this saying refers to our practice. The country is our life, and "prosper" does not refer to material riches, but to wealth of character. The king is our ego-grasping ignorance.

When the king is more important than the country, the country will not prosper. When the manager is more important than his or her employees, then the company will fail. If a manager is doing his or her job properly, then the company should run smoothly. The manager will become like a forgotten person, which is what a manager should strive for. Too many managers believe that they must have all of the answers and control every situation and take all the credit.

I became a very good technical manager. I knew how to manage up and down. You manage up by supporting your boss, and you manage down by creating an environment that allows those who report to you to succeed. As your boss succeeds, he or she will carry you up with him or her. As your employees succeed, they will lift you up on their shoulders. I was never afraid to hire someone smarter than me. I also put into practice one of Professor Isaacs's maxims: There is no limit to what you can accomplish if you don't care who gets the credit.

○

Julie and I found a house to rent when Michael took a position at the University of Michigan and sold his San Diego home. She got a job as a legal secretary, and with my salary we were in a position to buy a house, but we needed help because we did not have enough for the down payment. We were able to borrow from Michael, my sister Barbara, and a Mexican friend, Romulo Sanchez.

When I had been teaching in Mexico, I became close to Romulo, a Dharma drifter of independent means. He came from an influential Mexican family, studied economics at the University of Chicago, and started numerous businesses in his spare time. A lifelong seeker, Romulo spent some time at ZCLA, but his main interest was Tai Chi. He sat with me in Mexico City, and during my free days, he drove me to spiritual power spots in Mexico. Later, Romulo studied with Tibetan Buddhist master Namkhai Norbu. We kept in touch, and when I returned to Mexico after the turn of the twenty-first century, Romulo joined me again.

In 1990 Julie became pregnant again. I was forty-nine years

old and not prepared for another child. I thought that we had taken all the precautions, but this unborn being really wanted to join our family. We welcomed a little angel named Lily Romaine on December 4, 1990.

A few months earlier, Maezumi Roshi had talked to me again about receiving Dharma transmission and becoming a Sensei, an independent Zen teacher. This time I agreed, and we decided to perform the weeklong ceremony during the sesshin between Christmas and New Year's Day.

I lived in Maezumi Roshi's house, and we met every day several times to go over the documents and instructions. We did it in the traditional Japanese Soto style with all the trimmings. It was hard for Roshi to lead sesshin and to perform all of the transmission rituals simultaneously because both activities required his full attention. He said he could do it because I was not demanding and could go with the flow. It all worked out, and by the end of the week, with some help from Tenshin and Seisen, I was Shishin Sensei. I started sitting in our living room with a few people who wanted to study with me.

I still continued to assist Roshi with sesshin, and he always asked me to assist him with the transmission ceremonies for those who came after me.

Romulo Sanchez on the beach in Cabo Pulmo National Park, Baja Peninsula, 2008

O

My work at Action Instruments was beginning to get stale. I felt that the upper management was taking advantage of the employees and was arbitrarily cutting salaries and demanding longer hours. I started looking around and found an opening at Compton's NewMedia, a subsidiary of Encyclopaedia Britannica. The interview I had with Harold Kester, the chief technical officer, was the most amazing interview I ever had.

Somehow Harold knew that I was a Zen priest. (I did not feel that I could still call myself a monk since I had left the center, was working at a regular job, and was otherwise leading the life of a layperson.) I did not put it on my resume, but others from Action Instruments were also applying for the job and may have said something. Harold's teenage son had recently committed suicide, and it weighed heavily on his heart and mind. He took me out to lunch, and all he wanted to talk about was his son. He poured his heart out, and I held the space and shared with him for an hour. At the end of the hour he said, "You know how to program computers don't you?" I assured him that I did. Then he said, "You're hired."

Harold became a good friend and invited me to lead zazen in his house for him and some of his friends. He eventually took jukai and was a sincere practitioner until he died of cancer in 2005.

Harold Kester, 1994

I had plenty of time to tend to my children compared with when I lived at ZCLA. I taught Sam and David how to drive a car. Julie and I went on outings with all the kids.

Janna, Dan, and Lily, 1992

I spent countless hours playing ball with Dan, who turned out to be quite an athlete. I read books with Lily and taught her how to ride a bike. I helped all the kids with their schoolwork, including Julie's daughter Janna, and when it was time, I helped Sam and David select colleges and went with them on parents' day.

I had been ordained as a Zen monk and had not left home to join a monastery. The question about what it means to be ordained had been a serious subject of discussion at ZCLA. There were very devoted laypeople who did not want to take the vows of a monk and consequently would not get acknowledgment from Maezumi Roshi no matter how much they devoted themselves to practice. But I was living a life no different from that of a layperson. Zen had been my entire life, but now it was as if I had an avocation called Zen. Maezumi Roshi complained that I was not gathering more students and starting a center, but that would happen in due course.

Even though I was not spending as much time in a zendo, I felt that my Zen training continued to ripen in all of my interactions in the business world, at home, and at play. Every day was a good day. Like Layman P'ang, I felt that spirit-like understanding and divine functioning lie in *carrying water* and *chopping wood*. It also lies in earning a living and raising children.

○

In May 1995 Daido called and told me that Maezumi Roshi had died while visiting his family in Japan. The initial word was that he had had a heart attack while in a hot tub. But a year later I found out that he had been drinking with his brother Junyu and, drunk and exhausted, had passed out and drowned in the tub. Junyu had tried to hide the truth, ostensibly to protect Roshi's reputation; furthermore, Roshi's wife Ekyo did not want the children to be stressed by the truth. Bernie and Genpo knew how Roshi died but did not share the information with me. When I discovered the truth, I was very discouraged because this was the kind of secrecy that had led to the implosion at ZCLA. As a Dharma successor of Maezumi Roshi, I should have known the truth.

Maezumi Roshi was only sixty-four years old when he died. What a waste! What a pity! What an ignominious end! He had so much more to offer. I remember him saying that he could not establish American Zen; it was up to his successors to do that. Despite the waste and pity, I had a strong feeling that he had been ready to get out of the way and let us proceed on our own.

Like many of the Asian teachers who came to the West, Maezumi Roshi spent his teaching life spreading the Dharma to Westerners—he was able to make a heart connection with his students. He was both gentle and fierce when he needed to be. Maezumi Roshi's students were offered the best of both Zen traditions—the intense koan study of Rinzai and the silent illumination of Soto. The depth and influence of his training can be gauged by the diversity and influence of his successors, including Bernie Glassman, Genpo Merzel, Daido Loori, Joko Beck, and Chozen Bays.

Me, Joko, and Daido at ZCLA, 1980

My experience with Maezumi Roshi was that in the dokusan room, he was highly skilled in cutting off delusion and directing students to deepen their realization and practice. He had some character flaws, which have been well-publicized, but his primary focus never wavered from sharing himself and his understanding of the Dharma with his students. He was always accessible to those who were serious about their Zen practice. And now he was gone.

Chapter 10

SAYONARA JAPAN

A monk asked Joshu, "'The Supreme Way
is not difficult; it just dislikes picking and
choosing.' Isn't this a pitfall for the people
of today?" Joshu said, "Once someone
asked me about that and I haven't been
able to answer for five years."
—*Blue Cliff Record* Case 58

Just before he died, Maezumi Roshi had given inka, or
confirmation as a Roshi, to Bernie Glassman—and more.
So with his death, Bernie inherited all of Maezumi Roshi's
responsibilities. In his will, Roshi named Bernie as the abbot
of ZCLA. Before his death, Roshi had led a special sesshin at
Green Gulch Farm Zen Center in California to establish a
Soto Zen Buddhist Association (SZBA) that included senior
ordained students from Suzuki Roshi's lineage, Maezumi
Roshi's lineage, and eventually seniors from other American
Soto Zen lineages. Bernie was selected as president of SZBA,
and he also became president of the White Plum Asanga, which
is what we called Maezumi Roshi's lineage. Then there were
many dealings with the Soto school in Japan. And last, but
not least, was preparation for a massive memorial service for

Maezumi Roshi.

These responsibilities must have been the last things that Bernie wanted. He was deeply involved in developing the Greyston Foundation to eliminate homelessness in Yonkers, New York, and was starting to create the Zen Peacemaker Order. However, he was able to relinquish many of those responsibilities within a year.

First, there was the funeral in Japan. I did not go but chose to drive to ZCLA and meet with the shocked sangha there. We sat in the zendo, and I told them how lucky we had been to have lived in a time when we could study with someone like Maezumi Roshi. There is a Buddhist parable about how rare it is to be born human and to be born in a time when the Dharma is being expounded and to meet a qualified teacher. It is like a blind turtle in the ocean that surfaces every thousand years. A golden life preserver is floating on the surface, and the likelihood of the turtle putting its head through the ring is the same as the likelihood of all the conditions occurring that bring the Dharma into one's life.

During a day of tears and laughter, I told stories about Maezumi Roshi and invited others to share their stories. I said our practice was continually stepping into the unknown. Life and death are a journey into the unknown, and we don't know what will happen. As Master Jizo says in Case 17 of the *Book of Equanimity,* "Not knowing is most intimate." I invited everyone to examine their commitment to practice, to ZCLA, and to Maezumi Roshi's lineage.

Roshi's death was a great personal loss for me. Numerous occasions have arisen when I wanted his advice about how to deal with students and how to teach certain koans. The three major mentors in my life all died in their sixties: Roshi at age sixty-four, my father at age sixty-three, and Professor

Isaacs also at age sixty-three. I was fifty-four when Roshi died and had no Dharma heirs and no practice center. Because I did not expect to outlive my mentors, I felt as if time were slipping away and that I had only ten more years to accomplish everything. Wrong!

I had finished my formal studies with Maezumi Roshi and was an independent teacher and could carry on by myself. Others who had studied with him for many years were near completion of their formal training when he died. I called them Zen orphans. They had to find a new teacher if they wanted to continue. The most senior students migrated to Bernie. Wendy Egyoku Nakao and Anne Seisen Saunders studied with Bernie in New York and became his Dharma successors.

○

When Bernie, Egyoku, and the others returned from the funeral in Japan, they had several decorative packages with urns that contained Roshi's relics. (In Japan, the bone fragments in cremated remains are picked out by priests, disciples, and family members and kept as relics.) The major packages were to be placed in the founder's room at ZCLA and in his memorial site at Zen Mountain Center. Each of his successors also received a package and a memorial plaque. I have mine on an altar in my dokusan room next to his picture. Every morning when I offer incense at the founder's altar, I wish Roshi a good day and ask for his protection and guidance.

We had to sort through Roshi's belongings. Ekyo took care of the personal items, and I joined Bernie and Egyoku, who had been Roshi's personal assistant, to sort through the many Dharma items that he had left behind, such as various robes, ceremonial articles, calligraphies, and notes. Some became temple treasures of ZCLA, and others were dispersed over time to White Plum members.

Bernie, Egyoku, and Yoshin made plans for a monumental memorial service in Los Angeles that was coordinated with Japan. It took three busy months to work out the logistics and prepare the rituals. On the appointed day, we processed from ZCLA to important locations in Maezumi Roshi's life, such as the original zendo on Serrano Street and Zenshuji Soto Zen Mission. We ended up at the Japanese American Civic Center in Little Tokyo. I recall eulogies by Aitken Roshi and Father Robert Kennedy Roshi. Bill Jakusho Kwong Roshi, a teacher from San Francisco Zen Center, took Dharma questions from the audience. Roshi's young son Yuri asked him, "Where is my father now?" I don't remember what Kwong Roshi said, but I remembered that I had had the same question after my father died. I recalled the death poem of the rascal Zen monk Ikkyu: *I won't die. I won't go anywhere. I'll be here. But don't ask me anything. I won't answer.*

There could have been one thousand people at the memorial. Many of those who left ZCLA during the 1980s returned to honor Roshi's memory. Joko did not come, but her daughter Brenda Chiko and Joko's closest disciple, Elizabeth Yuin Hamilton, were there. The shadow sangha had its own gathering, and I made a point to attend to see how old friends were doing. I felt a kind of somberness at that gathering, but there was a lot of joy at Roshi's wake, which was a dinner and entertainment at the Civic Center. The next day many of us traveled to Zen Mountain Center for a service to place Roshi's relics in the gravesite there.

After things settled down, all of Maezumi Roshi's successors met with Bernie for the first meeting of the White Plum Asanga without Roshi. There were eleven of us plus

Bernie's successor the author Peter Matthiessen. The big question was would we be able to stay together, or would we fracture like other lineages have done after the founder died? Bernie tried to align White Plum with his efforts in Yonkers, but it was hard to align a bunch of independent Zen teachers whose empty minds were full of opinions. Within a year, Bernie handed the reins of White Plum to Genpo, who spent the next eleven years trying to keep White Plum together and to heal the wounds of our dysfunctional family.

$$\bigcirc$$

Before he died Maezumi Roshi wanted me to go to Japan to participate in a ceremony called *Zuise* where I would pay respects to Dogen and Keizan, the founders of Soto Zen in Japan. Part of the ceremony involves going to their original monasteries and being installed as abbot for the day. A Soto priest needs to have Zuise in order to be recognized as a senior by Soto-shu, the Soto school in Japan.

I was not keen to immerse myself in the Japanese forms, but to honor Maezumi Roshi's request, I decided to do it. Three other successors also wanted to do it. We arranged with Roshi's brother Junyu and with Bernie to have our ceremonies coincide with the one-year memorial service for Roshi in Japan. In May 1996, Charles Tenshin Fletcher, Nicolee Jikyo McMahon, Bill Nyogen Yeo, and I met in Tokyo to make preparations for our rituals. Bernie, Genpo, Egyoku, Seisen, Genro, and the official White Plum photographer, Peter Cunningham, were there and supported our journey. Chuck Lief, who took over as president of Greyston Foundation, was also on this trip. Not quite twenty years later, Chuck was selected to become the president of Naropa University in Boulder, where I taught for many years.

First we met at Sojiji, Keizan's temple on the outskirts

of Tokyo. Junyu forgot to tell us that we each had to come up with $500 to donate to the temple for the ceremony. Fortunately, there was an ATM machine nearby and I had enough funds to cover it. Then with some of the dignitaries standing behind him, Junyu told Nicolee that they could not find her papers so she could not participate in the ceremonies. I knew that since Maezumi Roshi was very meticulous about filing our Soto paperwork, something was amiss. When she objected, Junyu said she could come back another time and do it. What the hell!? She had already spent thousands of dollars to get there, to make arrangements to miss work, and to have her family cared for.

I was not going to stand by and allow these Japanese chauvinists to abuse the only woman in our group. As the senior member of our little cohort, I said to all the assembled Japanese Zen priests, "If you do not find her paperwork, I am not going to participate in these ceremonies either." I hoped that Tenshin and Nyogen would follow suit, but that ended up not being necessary. After the Soto administrators retired for a while, they miraculously found Nicolee's papers. That was a big relief, but whenever they lined us up during the rituals, Nicolee was always placed at the end, even though she was not the most junior of the four of us. We decided not to make an issue of that one.

One of my favorite koans is Case 42 of the *Gateless Gate.* In the first part of the koan a woman is sitting in deep meditation next to the Buddha's seat, and Manjusri asks the Buddha, "Why can a woman sit next to the Buddha and I cannot?" Buddha says, "Why don't you wake her and ask her yourself?" No matter how hard he tried, Manjusri could not wake the woman.

I have always thought that one point of this part of the koan is to teach the Zen monks to respect the abilities of women and to honor their Buddha Nature. This point seemed to have eluded the administrator priests that day in Japan. It is up to American Zen to help women find their rightful place, not only next to the Buddha's seat, but *in* the Buddha's seat.

I don't mean to imply that all Japanese Zen priests are chauvinists. I have met many wonderful Japanese Zen priests, both at ZCLA and in Japan. I just object to Soto-shu, the Soto Zen institution. While we were at Sojiji, busloads of the faithful came through for memorial services and deposited millions of yen into the coffers of the temple. I heard that they are told by the Zen priests that the more money they pay, the better rebirth their ancestors will have. But the word "Zen" means meditation, not payoff. Although we had many wonderful experiences on that trip, after it was over, I decided that I did not want to maintain relations with Soto Zen in Japan, directly or indirectly. I never took an interest in the Japanese Soto Mission in America or in the Soto Zen Buddhist Association and have never participated.

After we paid our $500, we were treated very well. We were assigned a monk who trained us in the ceremonies. We were given comfortable quarters, escorted to the hot baths, and ate wonderful meals. We had tea with the abbot, who gave us gifts of calligraphy and rakusu.

Eiheiji, Dogen's temple, was much more beautiful than Sojiji. It is deep in the mountains north of Kyoto and has a profound air of reverence for Dogen. We were able to enter the founder's room and pay our respects to Dogen. That occurs only during special ceremonies.

It was interesting to me that the ceremonies were not standardized in both of the mother temples. At Eiheiji the officiant turned to the right after approaching the altar, and at Sojiji he turned to the left. The kesa was worn differently in each place, and the officiating implement was different. At Sojiji it was a horse hair whisk and at Eiheiji a wooden stick called a *nyoi*. A few years later when I was teaching in Boulder, a serious Soto student complained that my ceremonial forms were wrong, and he left to find another teacher.

Hakuin wrote in his *Song of Zazen:* "Our form now being no-form, in going and returning we never leave home." That is a good koan. What is the form that is no-form?

As Joshu says in the epigraph: "Once someone asked me about that and I haven't been able to answer for five years." What is right? What is wrong? What is correct and what is incorrect? If you think you know, just wait five minutes or five years and it will change. Having opinions is not the problem. It is attachment to our opinions that is the problem.

After we were "Zuised," we spent some time in Kyoto with Paul Jaffe, the same guy who had taken Sam and David to the USC football game in Los Angeles years earlier. Paul had gotten a degree in Japanese studies from UCLA and was teaching at a Japanese university in Kyoto. As part of his thesis, he translated Yasutani's commentary on Dogen's *Genjokoan*. It is a marvelous piece of work that I have read several times. Paul was a great host, and it was wonderful to spend time with him again.

Back in Tokyo, we had the memorial service for Roshi. All six of his disciples who were present participated onstage. It felt like the end of an era. It was while we were in Tokyo that I learned the truth about how Roshi had died. I credit Nicolee for sensing that something was hidden, and she and I pressed Genpo for the truth until it came out. As I recall, it was also in Tokyo that Bernie handed the leadership of White Plum to Genpo. Genpo had remarried, and his new wife was able to help keep him out of trouble for the next twelve years.

○

Then there was the matter of ZCLA. Bernie flew back and forth between New York and Los Angeles trying to simultaneously care for ZCLA and Greyston. It was too much; he had to find a resident teacher for ZCLA, but none of the successors wanted to step up to the plate. Bernie came up with all kinds of schemes, including having me and Nicolee, who also lived in San Diego, be co-commuting teachers. Finally Nyogen Yeo, who described himself as a foot soldier in the Dharma, not a general, agreed to step in because of his love for Maezumi Roshi and ZCLA.

Unfortunately, within a year there was an incident involving Nyogen, alcohol, and two female students. After due diligence involving the White Plum, we all felt it would be best if Nyogen stepped down. Then Bernie asked Egyoku to fill the void. She had finished her studies with Bernie and received Dharma transmission. I happened to be in New York on a business trip at the time, and Bernie invited me to participate in her ceremony, which took place in Yonkers in a large nunnery that the Greyston Foundation had bought to convert into an AIDS hospice and treatment center.

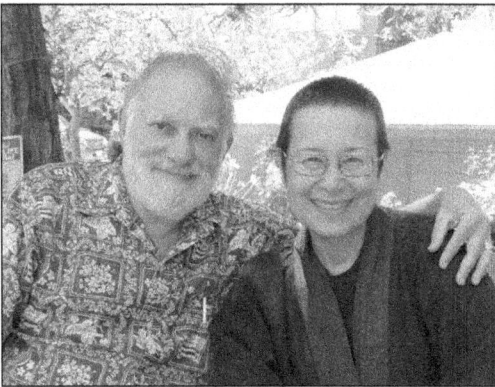

Bernie and Wendy Egyoku Nakao, 2015

Egyoku agreed to go to ZCLA for three months as a trial if she could do things her way. Bernie assented. With the patience of Job and the persistence of Sisyphus, Egyoku initiated the "circle process" at ZCLA—where everyone has an opportunity to have their say and to be heard. Now more than fifteen years later, Egyoku is still at ZCLA where Bernie installed her as abbot. She and the ZCLA sangha put in place many of the community forms that helped to heal the long-festering wounds at ZCLA and to create a healthy basis for continuing practice.

Bernie named Tenshin and Seisen, who had married, as co-abbots at Zen Mountain Center. It was a bittersweet time. Jishu, Bernie's wife and cofounder of the Zen Peacemaker Order, had just died in Santa Fe, so he was not able to attend the installation. I had known Tenshin and Seisen since they were "pups," and I was very moved by this new step on their path. I felt that they did a wonderful job stabilizing the Mountain Center, and when their paths diverged, Seisen left to establish Sweetwater Zen Center in National City just south of San Diego. Tenshin is still the abbot of Yokoji-Zen Mountain Center.

A strong force inside of me kept pushing me to set up a practice center and take on students. When the opportunity arose in Colorado, I uprooted my family, adjusted my livelihood, and headed to the Rocky Mountains.

Chapter 11

GREAT MOUNTAIN ZEN CENTER

> Students today should begrudge every
> moment of time. This dew-like life fades
> away; time speeds swiftly. In this short life
> of ours, avoid involvement in superfluous
> things and just study the Way.
> —Dogen, *Shobogenzo Zuimonki*

Dogen was always uncompromising. When he writes
"avoid involvement in superfluous things," I have to ask, "What
is superfluous?" He was a monk in a monastery. I couldn't
really call myself a monk. I was a householder. The word
"monk" comes from the Greek *monos,* which means alone or
single. I was more like a married priest. In general, a monk
is unmarried and devotes his or her life exclusively to the
Dharma. A priest can be married and tends to the affairs of a
temple by performing liturgy for the sake of the congregation.
I meditated, performed the Buddhist liturgy, *and* I worked
at a job and helped raise children. Samu is an important
part of monastic practice, but it is performed to support
the functioning of the monastery, not to maintain a certain
lifestyle. So what is superfluous in one situation might not be
superfluous in another.

A well-known Zen story involves monks from a monastery who were on their begging rounds. They walked in single file through the village carrying their begging bowls and wearing large straw hats that covered their eyes. This particular day, they passed a farmer whose cart was stuck in the mud; he could not budge it. One monk broke ranks and helped the farmer get on his way. When they returned to the monastery that monk was expelled for breaking the discipline of the practice. In Japanese Zen circles, the abbot is praised for teaching the monks that *time speeds swiftly* and to avoid *superfluous things.*

I was always bothered by this story. Where is the compassion? Recently I asked Bernie Glassman what he thought of this story, and he said, "It's terrible." But from the time of the Buddha, serious practitioners have always felt the conflict between time spent meditating and serving the Dharma versus the pursuit of other interests and involvement in daily life.

○

A few years before Maezumi Roshi died, I had started traveling regularly to Boulder, Colorado, to lead sesshin. I had been invited by Sumi and Colin Eagen, who were students of Roshi's, and by my brother Barry and his wife Padma, who had moved to Colorado. I think that my first Boulder sesshin was in 1992. It took place in a zendo that Colin and Sumi designed in their house. Each time I came, the participants became more involved, and eventually I thought there was a critical mass that allowed me to consider relocating to Boulder full time.

In this short life of ours, avoid involvement in superfluous things and just study the Way. I kept experiencing this feeling that my life was slipping away and I was not putting my energies where my destiny was calling me. I had been training my whole life to spread the teachings of the Buddha Dharma, and I had to go where the flowing waters of the universe were carrying me. They were carrying me uphill to the Rocky Mountains.

A number of factors had to come together to allow such a shift. First, I had to be able to earn a living in Boulder to support my family. In San Diego I had been working for Compton's NewMedia, which produced the first multimedia encyclopedia for computers. The parent company, Encyclopaedia Britannica, was a half-billion-dollar enterprise that still derived most of its income from door-to-door sales of its magnum opus, "The Big Book," as the encyclopedia was called. Compton's was a children's encyclopedia often bundled free as an incentive to buy The Big Book.

Into the 1990s, however, the Internet was undermining the profits in Encyclopaedia Britannica's traditional marketing channels. Search engines such as Google and then eventually Wikipedia, the free online cooperative encyclopedia, nailed the coffin shut on the company's book sales. To raise cash, Encyclopaedia Britannica sold Compton's to the Chicago-based Tribune Company, and I was part of the deal. Harold Kester, my boss, stayed with EB and created an Advanced Technology group to keep the company afloat. As part of the Tribune Company, I was promoted to vice president of technology. My department grew as we developed the encyclopedia for a variety of electronic platforms. However, the chief executive officer, Norm Bastin, was an avid music fan and wanted to produce CD-ROMs with features based on popular music.

I had met the musician David Crosby, of Crosby, Stills, and Nash, at a sesshin arranged with Michael O'Keefe, the actor-husband of Bonnie Raitt, who also attended. Michael was ordained in the Zen Peacemaker Order and was a devoted practitioner. Through David Crosby's agent, we explored creating products with David, Graham Nash, Ray Manzarek of the Doors (who was also interested in Zen), and Yoko Ono. We spent an afternoon with Yoko Ono in her Dakota apartment in Manhattan pitching a product.

None of this came to fruition, since Norm's ambitions ran afoul of the corporate culture of the Tribune Company, and they unceremoniously fired him. Shortly thereafter they let all of the upper management go and brought in their own people. I was out of a job. It was a relief to be able to walk away from the problems created by the clash between the Compton's culture and the Tribune culture. But I had no income, other than limited unemployment insurance, and a family to care for. I have great empathy for everyone who has ever been laid off from work and those who are being laid off now in our current stagnant economy and oligarchic political climate. I was able to land on my feet and find an even better job situation, but not everyone is so lucky. It is obvious to me that government and society have an abiding responsibility to take care of those who face adversity and are downtrodden.

When I was an adolescent, my father, who was a public service psychiatrist, took a job as director of the Arizona State Mental Hospital in Phoenix. There was a dusty baseball diamond on the hospital grounds, and my brother Alan and I would recruit some of the inmates to play baseball with us. We tried to make sides and play a real game. But we quickly learned that some of the inmates were uncoordinated and could not hit the ball; some who could hit the ball did not know that they were then supposed to run to first base; some got angry when they made an error or swung and missed the ball; and then there was the rare inmate who could really play with us, like Jack Nicholson in the movie *One Flew Over the Cuckoo's*

Nest. Nonetheless, it was the best we had and we made the most of it. We think that we both learned a lot about patience and compassion from those baseball games.

Years later, when Ronald Reagan was president, funding was cut to institutions such as the Arizona State Mental Hospital, and many of our baseball compadres and other inmates were turned out into the streets and became homeless. As a result, it is hard for me to pass a homeless person without thinking of my baseball teammates and wanting to help. During the 1970s the patient population of the hospital declined from two thousand to only three hundred. Fortunately, Dad was not alive to witness this transformation.

◯

Harold Kester came to my rescue when I became one of the unemployed. He connected me with the president of Encyclopaedia Britannica, who referred me to John Morse of Merriam-Webster, the dictionary company, which is a wholly-owned subsidiary of EB. I already knew John Morse since I had worked with him when I created an electronic Merriam-Webster dictionary to accompany the multimedia Compton's encyclopedia. John hired me to lead an incipient electronics products division at Merriam, and the best part was that I could work at home. Merriam-Webster is located in Springfield, Massachusetts, and I had an office in Harold's Advanced Technology group in La Jolla but rarely used it. I loved the freedom of working at home. The growth of the Internet made my virtual office possible. At that point, it was inconsequential whether I worked in California or Colorado, so one hurdle to moving was cleared.

Harold introduced me to a computer and linguistic genius named Chris Cole. Chris had a love affair with

Merriam-Webster and wanted to put the dictionary on multiple platforms and on the Internet. It was a battle with the conservative lexicographers at Merriam, but, as my legacy, Chris and I prevailed, and together we created the online version of the Merriam-Webster Collegiate dictionary. It is free, with revenue coming from online advertising. Unlike many traditional book publishers, Merriam-Webster survived because of Chris Cole's vision. Now more than half of the company's revenue comes from online products. I worked for Merriam-Webster until I retired in 2007 at the age of sixty-six.

○

My family had established themselves in Encinitas, the San Diego community where we lived. Julie was working for a lawyer who had become a personal friend. Dan had just finished sixth grade and was popular with his peers. Lily was ready to enter kindergarten. Janna was attending a local university. Sam and David had both graduated college and were starting their working careers in Los Angeles.

Julie told me to move to Colorado without her and Dan and Lily since they wanted to stay in California. But I did not want to be separated from my family again. I told Julie that I would not move without them, and since she did not want to keep me from my dreams, she agreed to go. Fewer than three years later, however, I broke her trust.

There was one more element to the family and the move: Julie's mother, Shannon, whom we called Grandma. Grandma was a deeply wounded person who had found her way to ZCLA in the late 1970s. Julie and Janna landed at the center because of Grandma when they moved west from North Carolina. Grandma depended on the kindness of others to survive in a normal way, and unfortunately she had alienated everyone in her life. The only person left who looked after her was Julie, even though Grandma regularly heaped scorn on her.

We had to find a place for Grandma to live that was not with us but was close enough for Julie to keep an eye on her. In years past, Grandma's family had homesteaded a section in the Hill Country of Texas near Junction, a small town that time had forgotten. When Grandma's mother died, Grandma inherited the family home and some surrounding land. She lived there by herself for a while until it was clear that someone had to help look after her. Julie sold the Texas inheritance, but it was not enough to find Grandma a place to live in California, so the tide was turning even more toward Colorado. I went there with Grandma to find a suitable place for her to live, and we eventually found a small house in the mountains in Pinewood Springs about a forty-minute drive from Boulder on the road to Estes Park.

When all loose ends were tied up in the summer of 1996, we made our plans, loaded our belongings and our dog into a U-Haul truck, and caravanned to Colorado. My brother Alan lent a hand with the packing and the driving. We arrived after three days and were met by our fledging sangha, who helped us to unload and get settled.

◯

The first order of business was to find a place for regular zazen. The relationship between Colin and Sumi had deteriorated, so I did not want to grow our new sangha in their home zendo.

I approached the Buddhist-inspired Naropa University in Boulder. Its long-timers had vivid memories of Maezumi Roshi from the time he had led their seminary while Naropa's founder, Trungpa Rinpoche, was on retreat. I had considerable support from Reggie Ray and Judith Simmer-Brown, who were senior students of Trungpa's and professors in the Religious Studies Department. With the blessings of Naropa president John Cobb, our Zen group started sitting in the Lincoln Shrine Room on the Naropa campus.

Later, when Naropa bought a new building on 30th Street called the Paramita Campus, John Cobb asked us to move our sittings there. He said that Trungpa had told him that new buildings needed to be "tamed" to purify their energy. Our zazen played a major part in taming Naropa's new building.

Naropa had a vibrant extended studies program during the 1990s, and I taught several courses and led meditation intensive retreats. I will never forget my first weekend Zen retreat at Naropa. I gave the information to the coordinator that it started each day at 5 a.m. and went until 9 p.m. When the publicity came out, it said the retreat ran from 9 a.m. until 5 p.m. I was obviously too intense for Naropa students. Even with the schedule cut back, it was still too much for most of them.

About that time, Reggie Ray asked me to be a regular adjunct professor and teach an annual course on Zen Buddhism. I agreed and taught at Naropa for fifteen years before I retired from academic teaching.

⭕

Fortunately, I was able to work at home, or I would not have been able to found a Zen center and provide leadership. After discussion with the sangha, we decided to call our new center the Great Mountain Zen Center to honor Taizan Maezumi. His Dharma name Taizan means Great Mountain. Being in the Rocky Mountains, the center seemed most fittingly named.

Then we set about incorporating and filing all the paperwork to become a legal entity. Julie took on that task as

Great Mountain Zen Center logo

Paul Gyodo Agostinelli, 2015

she had worked many years as a legal secretary and could decipher the requirements. She did an excellent job, and in 1997 Great Mountain Zen Center was born as a nonprofit religious corporation in the State of Colorado. We were recognized by the IRS as a 501(c)(3) tax-exempt organization. I set up a Board of Directors, and we wrote bylaws and were in business. Of the original board members in 1997, only one person remains in 2015: Paul Gyodo Agostinelli. Gyodo was resident at ZCLA in the early 1990s and has been my student for twenty years. I recognized him as an independent Zen teacher in 2015.

Every month we had a sesshin in a member's home. We moved from one member's house to another until we were able to finance our own place in 1999. One summer we rented a facility for a seven-day sesshin in Rollinsville in the mountains above Boulder. We sat in a yurt in the woods that was unbearably hot during the day and freezing cold at night. I had to conduct dokusan with students in a small tent down a mountain trail. Despite the hardships, it was the most powerful and most memorable sesshin I had with the Boulder sangha. It seemed like we were coming of age as a Zen sangha.

○

Sesshin in a yurt, Colorado, 1998

Beginning in 1995 when I started working for Merriam-Webster, I would fly to Springfield, Massachusetts, three or four times a year for staff meetings and to maintain face-to-face contact with those who reported to me. In 2002 Bernie Glassman through the Zen Peacemaker Order bought Montague Farm, which was about a forty-minute drive from Springfield.

For five years until I retired, Bernie and I spent time together during every trip I took east. We studied together and schmoozed and discussed Bernie's plans and my Dharma life. We became closer than we ever had been at ZCLA. For three years I was on the Board of Directors of the Zen Peacemaker Order, helping Bernie with his vision for Montague Farm.

I told Bernie how much I appreciated our close association and that my closest Dharma friends were all his successors. He told me that he had been thinking about giving me inka and the title Roshi. I readily accepted, to acknowledge our close relationship and to recognize him as my mentor. On his birthday, January 18, 2006, during a visit to Boulder,

140

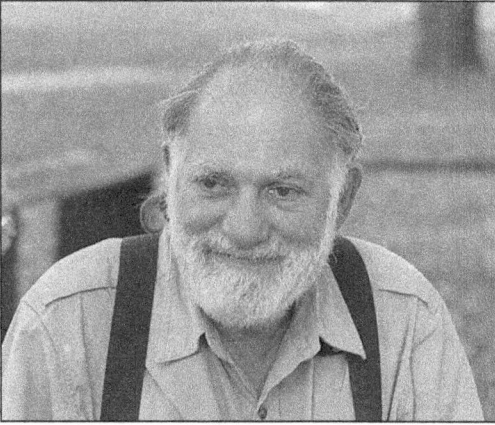

Bernie gave me a ceremonial rakusu and a poem in a public ceremony at the zendo of Great Mountain Zen Center and conferred on me the title of Roshi, or Zen master.

Bernie Glassman, 2012

Shortly after moving to Boulder, my lawyer friend in LA, Hal Stanton, called to tell me that his law partner, Norman Oberstein, had become the president and a board member of the Frederick P. Lenz Foundation for American Buddhism. The foundation had millions of dollars that were to be spent supporting American Buddhism, especially Zen. Hal had recommended me to their Advisory Committee to help identify worthy grant recipients.

Frederick Lenz, aka Rama, was a self-proclaimed Buddhist teacher of dubious repute. He had raised millions of dollars from businesses he developed and staffed with his students. I recall seeing full-page ads in the *Los Angeles Times* around 1980 promoting talks and workshops by Zen Master Rama. The Zen community does not look kindly upon those who assume Zen titles without the requisite training. Plus there were highly publicized scandals surrounding Rama. He died in 1998 under strange circumstances and left behind a fortune, which his attorney Norman Oberstein and his accountant Norman Marcus used to create the foundation.

The two Normans, who were Jewish, knew nothing about Buddhism and Buddhist organizations in the United States. Their Advisory Committee was loaded with Rama's students, and they wanted some diversity. I invited Daido, Bernie, and Genpo to participate with me. Daido thought that it would be bad karma and declined. Bernie wanted to see how things evolved, and Genpo signed up. The law requires a nonprofit philanthropic foundation to spend 10 percent of its assets every year. The Normans had money to spend and did not know where to spend it. During the first year, they put some funds into Genpo's Big Mind program and my project called the Great Heart Way (to be discussed in the next chapter).

I was able to funnel money to Naropa University for student scholarships, to support scholars-in-residence, and to support the university's contemplative education program. Through my efforts grants went to Zen Peacemakers, Zen hospice programs in Santa Fe and San Francisco, the Prison Mindfulness Institute of Fleet Maull, plus more. The foundation also supported several programs in the inner city that taught meditation skills to disadvantaged youth.

At the beginning Genpo and I took a lot of heat, especially from some members of the American Zen Teachers Association, which had formed in the late 1980s as a group of second-generation students who had received Dharma transmission from the mostly Asian early Zen teachers in America. Some argued that the money was tainted and we should not be promoting the likes of Frederick Lenz. I met a number of Lenz's students on the Advisory Committee and really liked them. They were sincere seekers of the Way. The Normans were honest and sincere and wanted to use the foundation's funds wisely. The only objection I had was that they wanted to promote Lenz and his writings and wanted all grant applicants to explain how they could incorporate Lenz's works into their grant projects.

I told the Normans that it was not appropriate to promote Lenz that way. I was rebuffed for several years until the Rama Meditation Society was formed by Rama's former students and became the conduit to support Lenz's teachings and works, which is the appropriate channel. The Lenz Foundation continues to foster American Buddhism through its charitable grants and does not actively promote Lenz's teachings. Feeling I had made my contribution, I stepped down from the Advisory Committee in 2010.

Philanthropic foundations that support American Buddhism are almost nonexistent. Eventually, the mainstream Buddhist community, including the ethical Insight Meditation Society, started to embrace the Lenz Foundation. In my exchanges with skeptics, I suggested that they take the money received from the foundation and put it to beneficial uses in order to transform their perceived negative karma of Lenz into positive karma.

Several Buddhist centers had taken money from the Rockefeller Foundation, even though, as I reminded them, John D. Rockefeller was a robber baron. He gained his money through ruthless business practices that took advantage of his competitors and his employees. In fact, Congress developed antitrust legislation starting in the 1880s primarily because of the monopolistic business practices of Rockefeller's Standard Oil. I asked my colleagues, "How long does it take for money to be cleansed?" Apparently, the Rockefeller Foundation money had been purified. Daido told me that had I made that argument earlier, he would have participated in the Lenz Foundation.

In his work *Shobogenzo Zuimonki* Dogen wrote: "Just

practice good, do good for others, without thinking of making yourself known so that you may gain reward. Really bring benefit to others, gaining nothing for yourself. This is the primary requisite for breaking free of attachments to the Self." This is how I tried to live my life. I tried to maintain the mind of service for those who came to practice at the Great Mountain Zen Center, for my family, and for my co-workers. But like Maezumi Roshi before me, I let down my family to follow my own personal spiritual practice and ambitions—and to pursue a new love.

Chapter 12

SHINKO

> Under the blue sky, in the bright sunlight,
> you don't have to point out the east or
> define the west anymore, but under the
> conditions of a particular time, it is still
> necessary to give medicine according to
> the illness. But tell me, is it better to let go
> or to hold still?
> —Engo Kokugon, Preface to *Blue Cliff*
> *Record* Case 4

Under the blue sky, in the bright sunlight, everything is clear. East and west are clear. Difficult and easy dissolve in the brilliant light. Effortless effort is manifest. And yet, this state of heart and mind does not last forever. Conditions of a particular time arise.

Working hard, sharing what I could with my Zen students, organizing sesshin, helping to raise children—all took their toll on me. I started to just go through the motions. At home, the TV seemed to continuously fill the space. At work, my view of how to move forward clashed with those in charge. At Great Mountain Zen Center, I felt like I was trying to squeeze out the last bit of toothpaste from an empty tube. I had uprooted my family to chase my dreams, and still I was not happy. What was my problem that I never seemed to find fulfillment?

Around that time, a cousin who was a physician told me that the Wick family had a genetic disposition toward hypertension, stroke, and heart attack. My father had a serious heart attack at the age of forty-eight; he survived another fifteen years by living carefully until a fatal heart attack took his life. My blood pressure, which had been low my entire life, started to creep up as I gained weight. Between sitting meditation, sitting at a computer, and sitting in front of the seductive TV, I did not lead a very active life. My one joy was taking walks in the foothills of the Rocky Mountains with Lily, who was then seven years old. She was the only one of my family who wanted to join me.

When I had been in top physical shape in college, I weighed 175 pounds. For most of my life I had fluctuated between 170 and 180 pounds. But when I stepped on the scale now, it read 210 pounds, and my blood pressure had crept above the healthy range. Something had to change. As Engo says in the epigraph, "under the conditions of a particular time, it is still necessary to give medicine

Alan, Barry, and me in Utah, 2001

according to the illness."

I co-opted a bicycle I had bought for Dan and started to ride it every day. At first I could ride only a mile, but after a couple of weeks I could negotiate the bike paths up in the foothills near where we lived. I stopped eating between meals and cut back on carbohydrates. The pounds started to fall, and I felt better. I lost about 10 pounds per month until my weight got below 180 pounds. Some days I would bike 25 miles, and I tried some of the strenuous roads in the area. My biking career culminated with a weeklong 250-mile bike ride in southwest Utah with my brothers, Alan and Barry, in 2001, the year I turned sixty.

On the third day of our bike tour, September 11, just after we climbed out of Zion Canyon, we heard the news of the deadly attacks on the Twin Towers in New York City and the Pentagon in Washington, D.C. We were biking in the high desert. The three of us stopped by the side of the road, and we built an altar in the cradle of a tree and chanted for those who had died and who were injured and suffering. I remember where I was and what I was doing the day that President John F. Kennedy was assassinated. And I will never forget the stark beauty of the spot where we built the altar along with the deep feelings of angst about how humans mistreat each other. It was a lonely, sad ride to Bryce Canyon where we camped for the next two nights.

After the bike ride, I rushed back to Great Mountain Zen Center in Colorado where a senior member, Ilia Shinko Perez, was holding the sangha together during those tough times. About one month before the attack on the World Trade Center, Shinko had had a vision of two towers surrounded by destruction. She made a drawing and a painting of her vision, which she had shown me before I left on my bike tour.

In the painting she drew herself praying for peace in a circle with others, with the devastation in the background. At Great Mountain Zen Center she had placed the painting in the middle of a sacred circle and chanted with the other members a prayer she had written. Shinko and I modified her Prayer for Peace, and we still chant it as a regular part of our daily liturgy:

> All Buddhas, Bodhisattvas,
> Protectors of the Dharma,
> And the Three Treasures,
> With all sentient beings
> I lift my heart to transform
> Ignorance, violence, and suffering.
> May healing and peace prevail
> Throughout the Dharma worlds.
> *Maha Prajna Paramita.*

> DEDICATION
> We dedicate the merits of this prayer to
> The flourishing of love in all countries,
> The healing of the earth,
> The peace of the world,
> The wisdom of the people,
> The compassion of our world leaders,
> And to the harmony of all beings.

Shinko had joined our sangha in 1997, and I had become more involved with her than I ever could have anticipated. She had been practicing Zen for more than ten years with the well-established teachers Philip Kapleau (who had written *The Three Pillars of Zen)* and Father Pat Hawk, a successor of Robert Aitken, and was an advanced student when I met her.

148

Ilia Shinko Perez, 1999

When Shinko came to practice with me, she was full of fire in a way that reminded me of myself about twenty years earlier. She constantly probed and questioned. In dokusan, I tested her understanding of the Buddha Dharma as best I could to make sure that she was not all bluster. Every Zen barrier I erected, she was able to pass through.

No matter how much I accomplished in my Zen journey, there has always been a part of me that yearned to keep deepening my meditation practice and experience more profound levels of understanding about myself and the world around me. Sometimes that longing had been dormant while I focused attention on the mundane necessities of life. When I first arrived in Colorado, it took all of my energy just to earn a living, to maintain a household, to help nurture my young children, to establish Great Mountain Zen Center, and to lead daily meditation and retreats. I was energized at first, but then I felt like I was in a holding pattern. With Shinko in my life, I was able to break out of that pattern and rekindle my love of the Dharma. Great Love arose between us that was grounded in our love of the Dharma. Engo asks: "Is it better to let go or to hold still?"

Julie and I had been married for more than fifteen years. We had many wonderful times together and had two beautiful children, who still lived at home. I was in constant turmoil

149

about which path to follow and where to turn. One day I would be certain that I had to cut off with Shinko since in my wildest dreams I could not imagine that I could break up my family. But the next day, the lure of being with Shinko and sharing the Dharma with her obliterated everything else. After a raging battle between my heart and my brain that lasted for several months, I finally let go.

Following the yearning of my heart and uniting with Shinko caused considerable pain for Julie and our children, especially Dan, who was fifteen years old. I was not straightforward and tried to hide my love for Shinko until it burst out into the open. Some wounds never heal, and I still feel remorse at how I treated Julie leading up to our split. In her heart, she probably understood me better than I understood myself and later summed it up by saying simply, "You fell in love with her." Although we went through some dark times, I will always be grateful to Julie for her generous spirit.

My Zen journey had been a long trek through uncharted woods and mountain passes. At times it had been a trudge where I laboriously placed one foot in front of the other. When I reached a vista point, the view was magnificent and certainly worth all the effort. Then the trudge continued. Shinko's Zen journey had also been difficult and laborious at times but interspersed with periods of great joy. When we met, she had been searching for her expression of the feminine on her Zen path. Since she had received no acknowledgment of the feminine path from her male Zen teachers, Shinko turned in desperation to a female Tibetan Buddhist teacher, who recognized her as a *dakini*. A dakini is a female who moves in space bringing enlightened teachings to men and women alike. She is a sky dancer.

When we started to share the Dharma together, my steps

were no longer heavy. I felt like a sky dancer. My teaching and my practice took on a lighter and yet more profound dimension. Dakinis also display a volatile and wrathful temperament as a means to invoke awakening. Having been raised in Puerto Rico and Spain, where people more readily speak their minds and hearts, Shinko was always close to her emotions. She was highly intuitive and clairvoyant. When she brought those qualities into her Zen teaching, they were not always appreciated by staid Americans, especially the macho ones. But those who were able to fly with her were amply rewarded.

When word got out to the Great Mountain Zen Center sangha that Shinko and I were developing a relationship, it caused quite a stir. By coincidence, Bernie Glassman and his wife, Eve, were in Boulder at that time. Shinko and I conferred with them, and Bernie recommended that we have a healing council with the sangha led by one of his students who was from Puerto Rico. In the fall of 1999, Paco Lugovina and his wife Noemi, who is also Puerto Rican, came from New York to lead a council at Shinko's home. Emotions ranged from support to skepticism to confrontation. In the end, some people left, but most stayed to support our nascent Zen center.

O

While bicycling in a neighborhood in Lafayette, about twelve miles east of Boulder, Shinko and I found a house for sale on Sparta Drive that could serve as a zendo for Great Mountain Zen Center. We were still doing daily sitting at Naropa University and sesshin in Shinko's basement not far from this house, but we needed our own place. The house backed against open space and Waneka Lake, around which we could do walking meditation during sesshin.

View across Waneka Lake, Lafayette, Colorado

We bought the house with my personal funds and money I had saved from teaching at Great Mountain. I moved into the house in April 2000 with one student. Shinko sold her house on the other side of Waneka Lake, bought the house across the street from the Zen center and lived there with her two sons, Lucas and Roldan. Soon we were having daily meditation and retreats at our new center. Sadly, the twelve-mile commute from Boulder was too much for some members, who stopped coming. A myth exits in Boulder that spirituality in Colorado does not exist beyond Boulder's borders. And one could not possibly awaken in Lafayette since it is a bedroom community devoid of enlightenment. I did not have the heart to tell all of the Buddhas and Bodhisattvas who live in Lafayette that according to Boulder's myth, they didn't exist.

At first we sat in the family room on the lower level, which could comfortably seat thirteen people; but we quickly outgrew it. The sangha got behind building an addition over

152

Snow Buddha at Great Mountain Zen Center

the garage for a larger zendo. One of our members, Christopher Melton, who is an architect, drew up a wonderful plan. With Shinko as the landscaper and interior designer, we built a beautiful new zendo using some outside contractors and much labor from the members, especially Richard Shinzen Blackmore, who was between jobs and able to devote considerable time to the project.

Members started to move to Lafayette and to Sparta Drive. During the first decade of the new century we had a thriving center and a sweet sangha. We held our first ninety-day ango in the fall of 2005 in the new zendo. And we have had an ango every year since. During the ango period a student is designated as the head trainee, which serves as a right of passage from being a junior student to becoming a senior student.

To acknowledge her Zen abilities and understanding, I gave Dharma transmission to Shinko on April 10, 2004, in a public ceremony at Great Mountain Zen Center. She was my first Dharma successor and became a Zen teacher, or Sensei.

O

The new century was a vibrant time for the Great Mountain Zen Center and for Shinko and me. In 2000, we traveled to Puerto Rico to meet two of Shinko's sisters who live in San

Juan. As Shinko recounted tales of her childhood, I soaked in the rejuvenating Caribbean water and air. Then we took a ferry boat to Santo Domingo to lead a sesshin. Our host was Joaquin Salazar, a friend of one of our students, Carlos Gento Estrella, who came from the Dominican Republic. Joaquin later became a successor of Paco Lugovina, our council facilitator, and thus joined the White Plum Asanga.

I will never forget the overnight boat ride from Puerto Rico to Santo Domingo. We reserved one of the four compartments on board. The rest of the passengers slept on the deck or in any nook they could find. They were primarily Dominicans who regularly commute between the two islands laden with merchandise that they buy and sell at each end of the line. It was like a modern spice road. That part of the Caribbean was a conveyor belt of cheap goods. Puerto Ricans, who are natural born U.S. citizens, could import manufactured goods from the United States. They would sell them to Dominicans, who transported the stuff to their island. The Dominicans would sell the modern goods to other Dominicans and to the Haitians, who were at the bottom of the food chain. Then cheap and crude Haitian handicrafts would make their way back up the trade ladder.

After leading sesshin in Santo Domingo, we received invitations to lead sesshin for budding Zen groups in Rapid City, South Dakota, and in Taos, New Mexico. Members regularly travel from South Dakota and New Mexico for sesshin in Colorado. We also have had members from the neighboring states of Wyoming and Nebraska.

○

For decades I had had the desire to write a Zen book, and the elements came together after I completed a series of talks on the koan cases in the *Book of Equanimity,* or *Shoyoroku.* An editor acquaintance at Wisdom Publications, Josh Bartok, who is now a Zen teacher, had been after me for years to expand the company's Zen collection. I had to severely cut my comments, or the book would have been 900 pages long and Wisdom never would have recouped their publishing expenses. As it was, the 320-page *Book of Equanimity* became the first book of modern commentaries on the entire collection of these koans; it has been well-received both by serious students of Zen and by those who have a cursory interest in koans. When I reread it, I am surprised at how good it is.

Shortly on its heels, Shinko and I collaborated on another book: *The Great Heart Way.* It should have been titled *Great Heart Zen,* which is closer to the point. As Zen Buddhism migrated to the United States, it took on at least three characteristics that distinguish it from the Buddhism of Japan, Korea, and other countries of origin: (1) a preponderance of laypeople practicing, in contrast to the preponderance of monastics and priests in Asia; (2) women and men practicing as equals, as opposed to women taking an inferior position, as in Asia; and (3) practitioners being more concerned with their emotional and psychological well-being as part of practice. That element is often ignored in Japan.

Japanese Roshis tell their students to avoid personal issues during dokusan and to limit the interactions to matters that arise out of their meditation practice. This was even though the great nineteenth-century Japanese master Hakuin had written that the most difficult part of practice is to take care of our "habit-ridden consciousness."

Shinko and I both acknowledged that we all have ingrained habits that subconsciously influence our behavior and choices in life and lead to suffering. Many of the problems that occurred at Zen centers around the country were due to teachers who may have had deep insight into the Dharma but shallow insight into their own habit-ridden consciousness. All of our students could benefit from insight into their hidden beliefs and habitual ways of behaving that cause suffering for themselves and others. Thus Shinko and I studied and experimented on ourselves and worked with close students to develop a way to use meditation as a means to uncover and transform our habit-ridden consciousness.

Neither of us is a psychotherapist, and we did not want to pretend to be doing therapy. But we discovered that just by sitting in meditation and staying present with strong emotions, new, informed insights can arise from the wisdom of the body. This does not involve analysis, although many of us certainly could benefit from analysis.

All of our work in this area was informed by our years of meditation practice. The Great Heart Way is a technique for using meditation to get in touch with the subconscious and help unpack the contents of its shadow side and eventually to transform negative patterns into beneficial ones. To paraphrase Carl Jung, meditation is the royal road to the unconscious.

Through the Great Heart work, I made a momentous discovery about myself. I knew that no matter how much I accomplished in life, I had an abiding feeling of not being good enough. I was successful in school, college, and university. I excelled in athletics. I became a Dharma heir of Maezumi Roshi and led my own retreats. Yet, an oppressive feeling kept tugging me down.

As I stayed present with that nagging feeling, images of my early Jewish education kept popping up. I focused on the story of Abraham and his son Isaac from the Bible, where Abraham prepares to sacrifice Isaac in order to show his fealty to God.

As a young boy, I had been frightened by that story and told myself that I had better be perfect or I would be sacrificed. In my child's mind, Isaac was spared because he was a good boy. I, on the other hand, was far from perfect; if I did not become perfect, imminent death awaited.

Through the techniques Shinko and I developed in the Great Heart Way, I was able to use my meditation to identify the sources of my self-doubt and to go a long way toward transforming them. I am pleased and relieved to report that I am now free from that oppressive theme, which had run me most of my life.

At the Great Mountain Zen Center, we added Great Heart retreats to our program of regular Zen retreats. Some students strongly resisted this new approach, and we did not force it on anyone. These retreats were quite popular for about ten years. We held them in Lafayette and then decided to hold them in more natural settings. First we went to Yellowstone

Me and Shinko, Great Mountain Zen Center, 2010

National Park along the Madison River, where we camped, set up a zazen canopy, and met in a meadow overlooking the flowing water. Then we held a couple of Great Heart retreats in Mexico on the Yucatan Peninsula. In 2006 we held a retreat in Tulum at the ecological reserve, and the following

157

Meditating at Lake Bacalar, Yucatan Peninsula, 2006

year we met at Lake Bacalar, which is close to Belize.

The retreat center at Bacalar was owned by Suzie Starr. Later I was invited to be on the Advisory Board of the Sage Institute founded by Sean Murphy, a student of mine in Taos, and Mirabai Starr, who by coincidence is Suzie's daughter. The Sage Institute is dedicated to bringing meditation to the masses, a movement I fully support, as I explain in Chapter 15.

The retreats in Mexico brought us closer to Romulo Sanchez, who was a close companion from the days I taught in Mexico City. Romulo attended our Great Heart retreats in Yucatan, and Shinko and I traveled with him in Baja California looking for retreat centers where we could teach during the cold winters in Colorado. Romulo owned property in Todos Santos near Cabo San Lucas at the tip of Baja California, and we seriously considered developing something together there. But then Naga came into our lives. Naga is a twelve-year-old mare of Arabian and mustang descent. Having a horse took us in another direction.

Chapter 13

MAITREYA ABBEY

> The hermit of Lotus Flower Peak held
> his staff up to a group and said, "When
> the ancients got here, why wouldn't
> they stay?" No one spoke so he himself
> answered, "Because it has no power on the
> Way." He also said, "After all, what is it?"
> Again he himself replied, "With my staff
> across my shoulders, minding no one, I go
> straight into the myriad peaks."
> —*Blue Cliff Record* Case 25

I must have been a fish in a former life. A fish has to keep moving to extract oxygen from the water as it flows over the gills. If a fish stops moving, it will die. Wherever I am, my piscine nature urges me to move on. I have had five different careers, three marriages (yes, Shinko and I got married fifteen years after we met), and I have never lived in the same place for more than a few years. The only thing I hold onto is my car, which I drive until it begs me to get another one.

If one remains in the same place in Zen, it is like a slow death. Even if one has a profound satori experience, it has to be released or it becomes putrid. As the Zen saying goes, "There is not a roof over your head nor a square inch of ground under your feet." The hermit of Lotus Flower Peak affirmed, if one remains in a fixed place or position, there is no power on the Way. So how does one avoid becoming stagnant and powerless? *With my staff across my shoulders, minding no one, I go straight into the myriad peaks.* Being free of all attachments, we go on like this.

The Great Mountain Zen Center had stabilized. We had regular programs and devoted members, and we were financially stable. A cadre of senior students could take care of the day-to-day details of running the center and could help prepare for retreats. I did supervisory work, but I mostly taught, and even that I shared with Shinko. It was time to shake things up.

Shinko had a horse when she was a child in Puerto Rico. She used to ride it bareback through the surf and recalls

Shinko and Naga, 2010

the freedom and exhilaration of her childhood with her horse. Then the realities of growing up and adulthood set in. Her horse died, and she thought that she would never adopt another horse again. After many horseless decades, Shinko started to visit horse-riding centers and took lessons to be able to mount, ride, and be close to horses. Then it happened.

Over the years Shinko had made many paintings that included a horse—usually a brown horse with a black mane and tail and a white streak between its eyes and nose. When Shinko resolved to adopt a horse, the first one we looked at was identical to the ones in her paintings. She was on the small side, standing about twelve hands at the shoulder. When Shinko saw her, there was an instant mutual recognition. All we needed was a place to board her.

We found a stable about a five-minute drive from Great Mountain Zen Center that had a vacant stall. It was affordable, and we could easily visit her and ride her in the riding ring. I knew nothing about horses. Like everyone else, I had only ever mounted an old trail horse when I was a kid. I didn't know a halter from a harness, and I didn't know how to act around a horse other than to be careful walking behind her.

Shinko named her horse Naga after the Buddhist deity who takes the form of a snake and guards the ancient secret teachings. Many ancient teachings are guarded by horses, and for the uninitiated, they are secret. I learned that horses are very different from cats and dogs. They have a huge bubble of awareness because horses are prey. Humans easily connect with cats and dogs since they are predators, and so are we. Being around Naga—feeding her, grooming her, and cleaning up after her—I learned about a whole new way of interacting with the world.

Over the years, I have been the custodian of many animals. I have adopted dogs and cats. I have raised chickens and kept fish and frogs and guinea pigs. For many years, I was an avid bird watcher with many bird feeders. But horses are a different breed. They are so sensitive they reflect one's state of mind.

In Zen we say that an untamed mind is like wild horses or wild monkeys. Try to approach a horse with your busy mind occupied with the dramas of life, and the horse will respond in kind. There will be no connection, and the horse will get agitated. To gain a horse's trust, you have to maintain an open, loving, and caring attitude. With willful horses, a trainer has to display confidence since they are herd animals and respond to the alpha horse. There is no place for abusive behavior, just assertive behavior.

Bearing witness to and appreciating Naga's energy and moods reinforced to me how important it is to connect with others without judgment. In the Zen Peacemaker Order founded by Bernie Glassman and his late wife Jishu Holmes, bearing witness is a crucial part of the practice. But it has to be nonjudgmental, or it just reinforces one's prejudices. When the Buddha was enlightened, he stated, "I and all beings are simultaneously enlightened." He was asserting that there is no separation between him and all beings. By bearing witness without judgment we began to realize the profound truth of that statement. Even those with whom we vehemently disagree are not separate from us. Even those from cultures that have beliefs and behaviors that are contrary to ours are not separate from us. Practicing meditation to realize this truth is an essential step toward world peace.

The manager where we housed Naga started to become careless about where he left building materials and barbed wire and thus endangered the horses. Shinko felt strongly that we had to find another home for her, and in the process we found another home for us as well. We started looking for properties that could accommodate a horse within a fifty-mile radius of Lafayette and found a neglected farm in Berthoud about a thirty-minute drive north of Lafayette and forty

What was to become Maitreya Abbey, before any improvements, 2009

minutes from Boulder.

The property, which is populated by numerous majestic poplar trees, was almost in foreclosure. The owners had not pruned a tree in years or cleaned the moldy, cat-pee-stained carpets. The fields were overgrown with weeds that reached more than four feet high. The roof of the farmhouse was sagging and in need of replacement. The only structure in good shape was the barn, which had been built only a few years earlier.

In Case 92 of the *Book of Equanimity,* Master Unmon says, "Between Heaven and Earth, within the universe, there is one treasure secretly dwelling in this mountainous shape." Everyone advised Shinko not to buy, but from the forsaken building and overgrown grounds was a magnificent view of the Rockies. She looked within and saw a secret treasure: a true Zen training center and a place to house Naga.

Long's Peak as seen from Maitreya Abbey

The price was right. With the sale of Shinko's house and a healthy withdrawal from my retirement fund, we were able to buy the 5.25-acre plot with the forty-five-hundred-square-foot farmhouse, barn, two falling-down animal sheds, dilapidated henhouse, and broken swimming pool. Now the fun began.

With the help of the sangha, and particularly Michael Mui Lewis and Billy Yuki Osipenko, we tore out every stinking carpet and put down composite flooring or tile. We removed the garish faux-Western paneling and painted all the walls. We converted one of the three garages into a resident's room and put a zendo in another converted garage. The capper was removing all three layers of shingles from the roof. I was going to pay a roofing company to do it, but Billy convinced me that sangha members could do it and save the center $4,000. We did it alright, but it took its toll. It was such hard work people were taking Tylenol as if the pills were part of a religious sacrament.

I think the roof removal cured some of our members of work practice forever. When I was at ZCLA, we would do whatever nasty job it took to help the center prosper and flourish. I recall a similar ugly task in LA when we spread

Samu on the roof of the abbey, 2010

hot tar on the flat roofs of the center's apartment buildings in the blazing sun. All of our members in Colorado have their own careers, families, homes, and other obligations.

As a consequence, Shinko and I decided that we would do community samu only during sesshin, and if we needed more work done, we would pay for it. I am deeply indebted to all those members—past, present, and sometime—who put their labor and money into improving the buildings and grounds of both the Great Mountain Zen Center in Lafayette and the new facility in Berthoud.

But before we did anything, we had to repair the fences so we could relocate Naga. The loafing sheds where she would hang out in harsh weather also needed repair. Two months after buying the farm, in December 2009, we were finally able to move in with Naga. A new neighbor graciously hauled her from Lafayette to Berthoud in his horse trailer, and she was home. Shinko moved to the farm full time, and I spent half of my time in Lafayette to maintain the programs at Great Mountain Zen Center. My first impression of living on the Berthoud property was that I was living in a drafty medieval castle. The cold winter wind whistled through the walls, and if we wanted to be comfortable, the heating bill was more than we could afford. It was four years before we had the means to upgrade the windows and doors and heating system.

Karma can work in strange and mysterious ways. I am reminded of the ancient proverbial rhyme "For Want of a Nail":

For want of a nail the shoe was lost.

For want of a shoe the horse was lost.

For want of a horse the rider was lost.

For want of a rider the message was lost.

For want of a message the battle was lost.

For want of a battle the kingdom was lost.

And all for the want of a horseshoe nail.

Our karma went in the opposite direction.

From a childhood memory, a horse was bought.

To house the horse, a farm was bought.

To support the farm, a retreat center was born.

To use the retreat center, the people came.

When the people came, they awakened their True Selves.

When their True Selves awakened, compassion arose.

When compassion arose, all people awakened and

Peace and tranquility reigned throughout the world.

All because of a horse.

At least that is my dream. It hasn't entirely played out like this *yet*, but we are on the Way.

Shinko wanted to name the farm Maitreya Abbey, after the future Buddha. Maitreya's name is derived from the Sanskrit word *maitri*, meaning "universal loving-kindness." Maitreya Buddha is the embodiment of loving-kindness. Infinitely compassionate and all-knowing, Maitreya teaches by words and example in order to guide us along the path to our own spiritual maturity. Because of Maitreya, my dream poem will be realized. Although Maitreya Abbey is not a monastery, we honor the noble silence and deep meditation characteristic of an abbey. Thus Maitreya Abbey was born.

Shinko organized and led programs at Maitreya Abbey, and

I did the same at the Lafayette Great Mountain Zen Center. In a public ceremony in July 2012, Bernie Glassman came to Berthoud and installed Shinko as abbot of Maitreya Abbey.

○

Horses are herding animals, so Naga naturally made friends with the neighboring horses across the pasture fences. But those horses were not in the pasture for all seasons of the year. When they were absent, Naga spent hours looking forlornly across the fence. Nobody wants an unhappy horse on their hands. So, we had to get another horse.

After looking all over northern Colorado, we found a large gelding quarter horse owned by Bruce Ford, a five-time world-champion bareback bronco rider. Bruce was the subject of the documentary *Colorado Cowboy,* which won the Cinematography Award at the Sundance Film Festival. He was a fierce competitor, but also a very nice religious man. He had just returned from church choir practice with his mother when we met him. Bruce told us that the horse we selected was very tame because he used to compete in rodeos running the barrels. I tried riding him since it was obvious that Naga would be Shinko's horse and Sky (what we named him because he is as spacious as the sky) would be mine. He immediately responded to all of my amateurish commands and won me over. Bruce delivered Sky the next week.

Me and Sky, 2010

As an aside: From holding the strap around the bucking bronco with his left hand for so many years, Bruce's hand was crippled and did not function. I had to help him open his pocket knife in order to cut the baling string from his hay bales so he could feed his horses. Such is the price of glory.

When Bruce delivered Sky, suddenly he was no longer the docile, obedient horse we had adopted. He immediately assumed dominance over Naga and beat up the neighbor's gelding, who had been showering attention on Naga. I didn't know how to handle a willful horse and had to take lessons on ground training and work in the saddle. This was taking more time and energy than I had anticipated! I started to feel tethered to the critters rather than free with my staff slung across my shoulders heading into the myriad peaks.

Since we had the room and already had animals, we might as well get more—or so the logic went. We adopted two rescue goats. One, a castrated male Namibian goat, whom we called Fauno (Spanish for "faun"), was slated for the barbeque pit before we saved him. Then we got Pixie, a female Nigerian pygmy goat, to keep Fauno company. Next it was chickens that we got from our neighbor, who raises rare breeds. When a patient raccoon massacred them, we built a henhouse and

Shinko with Fauno and Pixie, 2010

enclosure with double protection for our new hens, Rebecca and Claudia, who faithfully provide us with eggs. We adopted a shelter dog, a husky named Lola, to accompany our Australian shepherd, Toto, and a black cat named Kato (a pun on the Spanish *gato,* which means cat), who is a finely honed mouse killer. Finally, we dug a fish pond in which more than twenty koi and goldfish are thriving. (They do not yet have names.)

The animals provide a wonderful atmosphere during retreats at the abbey. Shinko had wanted to use the horses as part of a program to open participants' sensitivity to other creatures and to help them connect with their own internal energy. But we have not yet reached that point.

○

In the summer of 2010 we held a big fund-raiser at the abbey to remodel the half of the building where we were not living. There was a huge room that used to house an indoor swimming pool. The pool had been filled with concrete eleven years before we acquired the abbey, and the space could be divided into a zendo and a residents' kitchen/dining room/

Autumn at Maitreya Abbey after many improvements, 2014

lounge. The sangha and friends responded, and we were able to hire some workers to convert the swimming pool room and to add another dorm room and a workshop to the three-car garage that had been previously used for an auto-detailing business.

We were ready for retreats. Initially, we hosted all of the Great Heart retreats at the abbey and continued all the more traditional Zen retreats in Lafayette. Then Shinko initiated two new types of retreats: "Painting from the Unknown" and "The Sacred Feminine."

"Painting from the Unknown" embodies the same principles as zazen—being in the present moment, cultivating awareness without judgment, and finding the courage to step into the unknown. "Painting from the Unknown" is an enjoyable and challenging way of painting in which we don't have to worry about meaning, product, or goals. Amazingly, this kind of painting also embodies the same principles as the Great Heart Way—a heart-centered practice in which one needs to be in touch with one's feelings.

Periodically during the retreat, participants are asked the following questions:

- If I were free of judgment, what would I paint?
- If I were not afraid of what others think, what would I paint?
- If I didn't have to prove anything to anyone, what would I paint?
- If I could express my true feelings openly, what would I paint?
- If I allowed myself to feel embarrassed, what would I paint?

In the Great Heart Way as well as in "Painting from the Unknown," the words of Jesus in the gnostic Gospel of St. Thomas are great advice to follow: "If you bring forth what is within you, what you bring forth will save you. If you do not bring forth what is within you, what you do not bring forth will destroy you."

Painting from the Unknown

The "Painting from the Unknown" retreats are grounded in zazen, and from that space, participants explore their resistance and attachments to looking good and performing well. Just as in our zazen practice, a painting is never finished. We keep painting until the retreat is over, and amazing discoveries unfold. A strong inner force wants us to finish the painting and hang it on the wall to be admired. But even if a participant thinks the painting is finished and the retreat is not over, he or she has to keep modifying it. If you stay in one place, there is no power in the Way. Through the painting process we learn how to trust the creative force that surges from the unknown, and we are able to manifest it with strokes of brush and color on an empty paper.

The purpose of "The Sacred Feminine" retreats is to honor, to celebrate, and to bring forth the Sacred Feminine inside all of us. Shinko studied and intuited guided meditations, visualizations, and exercises to help both men and women balance their internal feminine energies.

We held these retreats for only two years before things started to unravel in Lafayette. We had to retool our approach to Zen at Maitreya Abbey. With our staffs across our shoulders, we went straight into the myriad peaks.

Chapter 14

White Plum Asanga

> You cannot hammer a nail into the
> empty sky.
> —The Record of Master Rinzai

In the spring of 2007, I was elected president of the White Plum Asanga, which is the organization of Zen teachers who trace their lineage through Maezumi Roshi. The organization was created in 1979 by Maezumi Roshi and Bernie Glassman, who were the first members; they named it after Roshi's father, Baian Hakujun (white, *haku;* plum, *bai*). Most people think the name is White Plum Sangha, where "sangha" means community, but it is White Plum Asanga. Asanga means "no attachment."

A cornerstone of the Buddha's teaching is *anatman,* or "no-self." The Buddha rejected the Hindu concept of *atman,* which postulates a self or soul that is eternal. Through his meditation, the Buddha realized that the notion of self is just that—a notion. When one looks deeply into oneself trying to isolate and identify an autonomous self, it keeps receding into the distance and can never be grasped. When one has "no attachments," one realizes "no-self." Attachments tether one to the world of suffering. "No-self" is like the *empty sky.* When one manifests that "no-self" as a continual expression of one's life, there is no place to *hammer a nail,* as Master Rinzai states in the epigraph. One does not get nailed tight to anything, including one's self. Everyone in the White Plum Asanga has experienced "no-self" to a greater or lesser degree. With a lucid realization of "no-self," it is clear that this "selfless self" is not independent and includes everyone and excludes no one.

After Maezumi Roshi died, everyone associated with ZCLA and White Plum pretty much wanted to go their own way. Bernie wanted to change the name to White Plum Sangha to emphasize the community aspect of our relationships. But "no attachment" had been too deeply ingrained in our psyches. For the first ten years after Maezumi Roshi's death, keeping the White Plum members together as a community was similar to nailing Jell-O to a wall, which is one step easier than hammering a nail in empty space. But it is doable.

When a student was recognized as an independent Zen teacher with Dharma transmission, he or she was able to participate in the White Plum Asanga. Maezumi Roshi had twelve successors before he died: Bernie Glassman (Massachusetts), Dennis Genpo Merzel (Hawaii), Charlotte Joko Beck (deceased, 2011), Jan Chozen Bays (Oregon), John Daido Loori (deceased, 2009), me (Colorado), John Tesshin Sanderson (Mexico City), Alfred Jitsudo Ancheta (New Mexico), Charles Tenshin Fletcher (Zen Mountain Center, California), Susan Myoyu Andersen (Wisconsin and Illinois), Nicolee Jikyo McMahon (San Diego), and Bill Nyogen Yeo (Los Angeles). If Maezumi Roshi had lived two more years, both Wendy Egyoku Nakao (ZCLA) and Anne Seisen Saunders (San Diego) would have been his successors. Both of them finished their studies with Bernie Glassman and are on his branch of the White Plum tree.

Front row (*left to right*): Tesshin, Maezumi Roshi, Chozen. Back row: Bernie, me, Daido, Genpo, 1992.

There are currently more than 120 members of the White Plum Asanga worldwide, all springing from these twelve. In some branches of the White Plum Asanga, there are four generations of Dharma successors. White Plum Zen centers are located in twenty-three states in the United States, eight countries in Europe (France, Belgium, Poland, Switzerland, England, Germany, Spain, and Holland), two countries in Latin America (Mexico and Brazil), and in New Zealand and Australia.

When Maezumi Roshi was alive, he was the president and spiritual director of White Plum Asanga. At our annual meetings, he wanted to spend time with further teachings, especially of the writings of the thirteenth-century Zen master Eihei Dogen, the founder of Soto Zen in Japan. We also spent time discussing organizational structure. Roshi and Bernie asked me to draw up a constitution for White Plum Asanga based on Soto-shu, the Soto Zen organization in Japan. It included three branches like the U.S. government: administrative, legislative, and judicial. The content was about standards for promoting and maintaining the Buddha Dharma. Ultimately, each Dharma successor would have a curriculum of study including face-to-face encounters with his or her teacher. The judicial branch would adjudicate potential problems that arose in the various sanghas. I wrote a first draft that was not finalized before Maezumi Roshi died in 1995.

Per the terms of Maezumi Roshi's will, Bernie took over as president of the White Plum Asanga. He tried to refine and implement the constitution I had written and to structure White Plum according to his own vision. Bernie excels at organizational structure, and I think he was trying to synchronize the direction of White Plum with his work at Greyston Foundation. Had his energies not been so divided, I believe that Bernie could have served with distinction and also could have filled the role of spiritual director of White Plum. Since it was not an easy task to align the members to his goals, Bernie stepped down as president and handed the reins to Genpo Merzel after one year and did not participate in White Plum much for ten years, although he was always available for consultation.

In contrast to Bernie, Genpo was not much of an organizer. For most of his tenure I was a vice president and treasurer of White Plum and Seisen was secretary. Seisen and I, often with the support of Genpo's wife, Stephanie, had to organize the annual meeting, which was held in Salt Lake City while Genpo was president.

Genpo has a compelling blend of conflicting personalities. He is both narcissistic and compassionate. In one moment he can embrace you with his charm, and in the next he can try to exert control over you. His exploits as a womanizer are well-

White Plum meeting in Salt Lake City, 1998, with me in the front and (*left to right*) Tenshin, Chozen, Daido, Genpo, Jitsudo, and Myoyu

known. Underlying all that is his deep love for and trust in the Dharma. Maezumi Roshi sent Genpo to Europe to establish the White Plum lineage there. Genpo left an enduring legacy in France, Holland, Poland, Germany, and England, with accomplished successors and devoted students. When he took over the reins of White Plum, he had returned from Europe and was living in Salt Lake City. As I see it, his role for the next ten years was to keep the White Plum Asanga intact and prevent it from fracturing like Yugoslavia did after the death of Tito. That was his vow to Maezumi Roshi.

In our annual White Plum meetings, we spent the ten years of Genpo's tenure processing all the hurts and wounds that we had felt when we trained together under Maezumi Roshi. Like any family with an alcoholic father, many dysfunctional relationships existed among us. This process was relevant to those members who actually studied at Zen Center of Los Angeles and lived in the community there. When new members joined, they often wondered what we were talking about. Chozen was always pushing for a strict code of ethics, and almost twenty years later, the organization developed a code of ethics and a grievance procedure. Like good Mahayana Buddhists, we created a code that is not strict but flexible according to circumstances.

Two times in the 1990s a member was censured for abuse of power and asked to suspend his teaching duties, seek psychological help, and make reparation for the damage he caused. Both dropped out of White Plum Asanga, although one was reinstated later. Since one of the aggrieved students threatened to sue White Plum Asanga unless we publicly rebuked her teacher, we decided that we had to change the legal structure of the organization to protect the officers and members from lawsuits.

We are now an affinity group or collegial group with no legal ties to each other. Membership is no longer automatic after someone receives Dharma transmission in the lineage. The White Plum lineage, as distinct from the White Plum Asanga, includes everyone, even Joko Beck, who broke with Maezumi Roshi shortly after receiving Dharma transmission. A qualified person has to apply for membership in White Plum Asanga, and that membership can be revoked for no cause. Thus far, this has happened only in cases of inappropriate behavior.

When Genpo became president, the question of a spiritual director of White Plum had not been resolved. Maezumi Roshi obviously had been the original spiritual director, and members were willing to accept Bernie in that role when he was president. Genpo wanted to be spiritual director and the teacher of the teachers. He assumed that mantle although it had not been granted to him. At White Plum meetings, he started imposing on those present his "Big Mind Process," which he had developed and which merges Buddhist and Western psychological ideas and techniques.

Big Mind is based on Voice Dialogue therapy, which was created by Hal and Sidra Stone. The Stones came to ZCLA in the 1980s to support the community's healing after the revelation of Maezumi Roshi's inappropriate behavior. Genpo adapted their work to provide what he calls a "quick path to enlightenment." Using his charm, charisma, and native intelligence, Genpo was incredibly successful with his Big Mind program. He made big money, in contrast to most Zen centers, which barely eke by.

Big Mind certainly has some value, particularly if it inspires someone to engage in a serious meditation practice. Some of the White Plum teachers close to Genpo use it as a supplement to zazen. But all of us felt that Genpo was taking advantage of a ready audience by trying out his latest Big Mind schemes during White Plum meetings without the permission or approval of those attending.

"Mindfulness meditation" is currently making a moderate splash in the media and in various parts of society. It is being used as a technical approach to solving problems and for gain and profit. These are not the purposes that the Buddha intended. Some serious practitioners derisively call these approaches and claims "McMindfulness," after the fast-food chain McDonalds. Many of us saw Big Mind in that light. However, I have come to the conclusion that any type of meditation is ultimately good for society. (I will explain more in the next chapter.)

Just before Maezumi Roshi died, he had completed all

the papers for Bernie to receive inka. Inka is the highest acknowledgment possible in Zen, and with it one can claim the title Roshi, or Zen master. Genpo received inka from Bernie, and Daido Loori received inka from Genpo. Later, I received inka from Bernie, and Chozen, Tenshin, Myoyu, and Jikyo all received inka from Genpo in a mass ceremony during a White Plum meeting.

Excluding Joko, Daido was the oldest of Maezumi's successors. He died in 2009 at the age of seventy-eight; Joko died in 2011 at the age of ninety-four. When we lived and practiced together at ZCLA, Daido and I were very close friends. He was a navy veteran, a chemist, a photographer of some repute, and an Italian through and through. We worked and played together; he was like a brother to me.

In his earlier Zen days, Daido was quite a rebel. He disliked liturgy and always skipped out of the zendo when chanting services began to smoke a cigarette in the back garden. He complained to Maezumi Roshi that we were doing *Japanese* ceremonies rather than *Buddhist* ceremonies. Roshi had no patience for that kind of talk.

In 1979 when Bernie went to New York to establish the Zen Community of New York, Daido and his wife Joan Yushin and son Asian went with him. Daido, the rebel, lasted about one year with Bernie when he found a Catholic monastery for sale for cheap in upstate New York. Always wanting to be independent, he scraped together enough money to buy the property and establish Zen Mountain Monastery one year short of his fiftieth birthday. There was one big problem: Daido had not finished his studies with Maezumi Roshi or Bernie in order to be an independent Zen teacher.

Maezumi Roshi decided to support Daido and took over the titular reins of Zen Mountain Monastery while Daido

continued to study with him. Genpo and I also helped
train Daido with his koan studies until Maezumi Roshi felt
comfortable giving Dharma transmission in 1986. With the
help of a Japanese monk, Dosho Saikawa, who had lived at
ZCLA, Daido put the Zen forms in place for Zen Mountain
Monastery. The ironic thing is that the rebel established the
most traditional and rigid training center of any of the White
Plum members. In the early days, I led seminars and retreats at
Zen Mountain Monastery to help Daido get on his feet. With
his flair for marketing and organization and through the sheer
weight of his playful, yet stern, personality, Daido was not only
able to make a go of it, but eventually to thrive.

Daido was an active member of White Plum Asanga until
it started to grow. Then he withdrew his participation from
the meetings. Most of the members were adapting Zen to
the American culture, and, at least for the Zen training part,
Daido was a traditionalist and very stubborn about it. I will
never forget the ads he placed in Buddhist magazines calling
Zen Mountain Monastery "Authentic Zen." Some of us joked,
"What are we?—inauthentic Zen?" Who was the true rebel
with no rank?

Daido and I remained close friends until his death. I saw
him a few weeks before he died of lung cancer after a lifetime of
smoking. I offered the following poem at his memorial service:

> Daido my friend, my Dharma brother,
> Old Salt in a rakusu.
> Throughout the Dharma realm, nothing escaped your lens.
> Relentless in kindness, you exposed your heart and guts.
> Never wordless, you expressed the silence of the mountains.
> Always stubborn, who can call you a blind donkey?
> Beyond right and wrong,
> Vastly clear, attachments left behind.

Memorial service for Maezumi Roshi at ZCLA, 2007, celebrating the center's fortieth anniversary. Front row (*left to right*): Father Robert Kennedy Roshi, Myoyu, Tenshin, me, and Chozen.

Alone, you stand everywhere, leaving no traces.

With rounded shoulders, you're content to go on like this.

You are still in our hearts. And we release you to be
    utterly free.

Gate, gate, paragate, parasamgate, bodhi svaha.

Gone, gone, gone beyond, gone beyond to the other shore.

At the 2007 White Plum Asanga meeting during the fortieth anniversary celebration of ZCLA, I was elected president when Genpo decided to step down. I served for six years and tried to get more people involved and to flatten the hierarchy. If we were to be an affinity group and an organization built on the foundation of "no attachment," then we needed to get rid of distinctions of senior and junior, which is tricky when the relationship between some members is that of teacher-student.

When I first came to ZCLA, a plaque inscribed by Maezumi Roshi hung outside the zendo that read:

Those who wish to realize and actualize the Buddha's Way are welcome. Otherwise you better keep out.

Let us be harmonious like milk dissolved in water. Temporarily, there are the relationships of guests to master and juniors to seniors; however, eventually all of us will be Buddhas forever. We should maintain the Buddha-Mind, moment after moment.

Let us not waste time. Time flies swiftly and nothing is dependable. Reflect upon the transiency of our lives.

Do not blame or criticize others. Do not imitate the falsehood of others, but nourish your own virtue. Correct errors and do not hate them.

Pertaining to the zendo, necessary matters will be discussed with the Master. When the decorum of the guests and master relationship gets out of order, absolute and relative functions will not be actualized.

No talking is allowed in the zendo. No strong scent such as perfume is allowed. Do not walk in the zendo with your hands at your side.

Be at home and be comfortable. Let us be respectful to ourselves and others, as well as to the Buddha.

Our zazen is the zazen of Buddhas. Transcending both enlightenment and delusion; let us be aware of this very fact.

Let us be selfless and be ourselves and accomplish the Great Four Vows together.

Maha Prajna Paramita,

Taizan Hakuyu (Maezumi), Gassho [1968]

Temporarily, there are the relationships of guests to master and juniors to seniors; however, eventually all of us will be Buddhas forever. That was the spirit with which I tried to lead the White Plum Asanga. There was no junior and no senior, and no attachment to position—just Buddhas interacting forever.

During my tenure, we cleaned up the bylaws that define the organization and posted a code of ethics as well as started work on a grievance procedure when complaints against a member escalate to the White Plum Asanga. The officers and Board of Directors felt we needed to do something substantial in this area after Genpo publicly acknowledged once again, after a twelve-year hiatus, that he had had sexual relations with several of his students. I wanted Genpo to work within the White Plum Asanga to address his issues of abuse of power, but he chose to resign from the organization instead and to do it his own way.

The following is from an article written by Sean Murphy, "Keeping Zen Alive," that appeared in *Tricycle* magazine (Fall 2009). Sean, who was a student of Daido's and now studies with me, was a guest at the 2008 White Plum meeting held in Santa Fe at Upaya Zen Center led by Roshi Joan Halifax:

Although the White Plum was originally organized along traditional hierarchical lines, it has changed its mandate in recent years. President Gerry Shishin Wick emphasizes that the organization is currently structured as an affinity group, in which any formally sanctioned teacher in Maezumi's lineage can choose to join—or not—and everyone has an equal voice. "We're not a sanctioning agency," explains Shishin Roshi, "but a community of peers." What he doesn't say is how revolutionary this is. A dharma organization operating outside of seniority, title, or gender roles would have been virtually unheard of through most of Buddhist history. Although, as anyone can see from the informal tone of this first night's gathering, the attire ranging from monastic black to blue jeans, and the gender balance of 18 women and 17 men, the revolution has already occurred.

In the years since Maezumi Roshi's death, each meeting of the White Plum Asanga has had to deal in some way with serious questions of how—and sometimes whether—to go forward as a sangha. For many of those present, this feels like the first meeting in which such concerns no longer dominate. There is a newfound sense of freedom, with past troubles and conflicts laid to rest. Several participants point to the joy of simply coming together so openheartedly; of the great gift of sharing the dharma face-to-face.

Chapter 15

NEW DIRECTIONS

> Obaku said to a crowd, "You are all
> gobblers of dregs. If you go on like this,
> where will you have today? Don't you
> know that there are no Zen teachers in all
> of China?" Then a monk came forward
> and said, "Then what about those who
> teach followers and lead communities
> all over the place?" Obaku said, "I don't
> say there is no Zen, just that there are no
> teachers."
> —*Blue Cliff Record* Case 11

I have been teaching Zen for more than thirty years, and
yet Obaku says that there are no Zen teachers. It is said that
Zen is a path beyond words and letters that points directly to
the human heart. Teachers impart knowledge. The common
understanding is that knowledge is something that exists
independently and externally from oneself and that we can
learn it through study. This kind of understanding posits a
duality between knowledge and the knower. Zen is a path of
nonduality, and Zen understanding is more a state of being, of
realizing our essential nature before thinking about it. It is like

awakening from a dream and experiencing our long-lost home. The great quantum physicist Erwin Schrödinger intimately recognized the nondual nature of reality when he wrote that one's self "is identical with the whole [universe] and therefore cannot be contained in it as part of it."

At the deepest level, there can be no Zen teacher and no Zen students. Not because it is impossible for a teacher to guide a student, but because when the teaching relationship is actualized, there is no gap between the two people and they both disappear into the space of the relationship. Teacher and student are one. To fulfill my vows as a Zen teacher, I use all my skillful means to guide students to that place of "no separation." That would be no separation not only with their teacher, but no separation within themselves. They have to see and embody their interconnectedness with all creations and all things. Not everyone is willing to take the risk or has the courage to realize this nonduality. It requires letting go of all cherished opinions and attachments.

There is always a point in one's practice where strong resistance comes up. It has happened to me on numerous occasions. But my faith in the Buddha Way and my trust in my own process provided the guiding lights to bring me through the darkness. Not everyone has the same determination and conviction that I do. I profoundly learned that lesson when a number of long-time students departed in 2012 and 2013, leaving a crumbling skeleton at the Great Mountain Zen Center in Lafayette.

Everyone has his or her own story. Some blame me, some blame Shinko, some blame both of us. Some just ran out of steam. I always tried my best to bring a student to awakening and never wanted to harm anyone. But in the eyes of some, I fell short. I don't say there is no Zen, but there are no Zen teachers. Zen means seeing fearlessly into one's true nature and relating to the true nature of all phenomena without a thought of separation arising. When one realizes Zen, one's behavior necessarily changes. Rather than projecting our discomfort onto someone else, we take complete responsibility for our actions and reactions.

A Mahayana text says: The True Mind of every sentient being teaches and leads each sentient being by itself. This is the vow of Buddha.

In our own minds we create all kinds of illusions that don't have any substance. We create a true self, a false self; we create enlightenment, we create delusion. We create all kinds of projections about our fears. Whatever feelings we have, we rationalize them and we justify them. When we meditate, one of the things we have to learn is that when desires come up, we can leave them alone without fulfilling them. Because we have a desire doesn't mean that we have to fulfill it. Because we see something, or because it's in our mind doesn't necessarily mean that it's there. From the side of the True Mind viewing the conditioned mind, we see how far we really have to go, how inadequate, in a way, our understanding and our practice are. In viewing the True Mind from the conditioned mind, we have a direction to go. So the True Mind is our teacher. The more clearly we see it, the more clearly it reveals to us the true direction.

When one of his students was complaining about how he did not set a proper example, Achancha, a Buddhist teacher said:

> Yes, it is true, a teacher should set an example for his disciples. I don't mind that you criticize me. Ask whatever you wish, but it is important that you do not cling to the teacher. If I were absolutely perfect in

outward form, it would be terrible. You would all be too attached to me. Even the Buddha would sometimes tell his disciples to do one thing and then do another thing himself. Your doubts in your teacher can help you. You should watch your own reactions. . . .

Wisdom is for you to watch and develop. Take from the teacher what is good. Be aware of your own practice. If I am resting while you all must sit up, does that make you angry? . . .

One of my teachers ate very fast. He made noises as he ate. Yet he told us to eat slowly and mindfully. I used to watch him and get very upset. I suffered, but he didn't! . . .

Looking outside the self is comparing, discriminating. You will not find happiness that way. Nor will you find peace if you spend your time looking for the perfect [person] or the perfect teacher. The Buddha taught us to look at the dharma, the truth, not to look at other people.

Students often go through a series of stages when relating to their teacher. First is always skepticism until trust is established. Second is idealization of the teacher as the perfect being. Third is demonization when students learn that the teacher has human foibles. They get frustrated with practice and start to project their negative biases onto the teacher. Often the relationship is mutually abandoned at this point. If students can see through their resistance to practice and projections on the teacher, the next phase can be realized. In the words of my Dharma sister Roshi Joan Halifax:

There's a relationship that's based on differences in capacity, but also upon a kind of equality. We project our enlightenment upon our teachers; we also project our negative qualities onto our teachers. What we need to do is to understand that process in order to enter into a more normalized relationship with our teacher. You care about your teacher, the well-being of that person, just as you would care for your grandmother or your parents. And your teacher cares about you. There's a kind of intimacy and love there that is very important.

I have experienced that intimacy and love with my teacher, Maezumi Roshi, and with a number of my students. Unless students can cease projecting negativity onto their teachers, they will leave that meditation practice. If they find a new teacher, they will play out the same scenario until they can transition to a more healthy relationship. One of my students stopped meditating for twenty years when he became discouraged. When he returned, he was the most devoted of all. After sitting with me for more than ten years, he succumbed to his weak heart, which had undergone several operations. He meditated diligently until the end of his life. I crave students with that kind of devotion to the Way of the Buddha.

Shinko and I did put pressure on a couple of students who had been with us for a long time. They chose to leave rather than work through their issues with us. A couple of long-time members preferred to find relief from the stress of life in their addictive behaviors of drinking and smoking rather than to continue exploring their Zen path. Others experienced significant changes in their life situations, such as pregnancy or leaving town to pursuing a working career.

When the dust had settled, about seven of ten core members left the Great Mountain Zen Center. It was sad because we no longer had the support necessary to maintain both the Zen center in Lafayette and Maitreya Abbey in Berthoud. It seemed like a rare event for so many long-time students to abruptly and almost simultaneously turn about face and march out of the Zen center. If I were an astrologer, I would say that a very rare celestial event occurred that year. In fact, there actually was a rare occasion in May 2012 when the Earth, the sun, the moon, and the Pleiades aligned to create great forces of transformation. It was a time of information overload, when minds became clouded as dreamy Neptune made a stressful square to the New Moon.

Of course, there is the more prosaic explanation that our students just lost faith in us as teachers and wanted to find their True Mind elsewhere. But as Obaku says in the epigraph, "If you go on like this, where will you have today?" If you keep looking outside yourself, how will you ever find self-realization and inner peace?

We had no choice but to sell the Zen center in Lafayette and develop the abbey into a Zen retreat center. When we announced the sale, most of the push-back came from those who had not been participating but liked the idea of having the Zen center in Lafayette. But their good intentions and lack of

Eye-opening ceremony for new Buddha at Maitreya Abbey, 2014

190

participation were not enough to keep the Zen center afloat. We had the final sesshin in Lafayette in June 2013 and sold the property a few months later. With the funds we were able to renovate the abbey so that those attending sesshin would be more comfortable there. I will continue teaching Zen wherever that may be until I no longer have the strength to climb up on my meditation cushion.

O

On July 28, 2012, Shinko and I got married. We had been living and teaching together for more than a decade. In the backyard of Maitreya Abbey a large apple tree was particularly abundant that year. Shinko constructed a thirty-foot cloth snake filled with balloons and draped it through the branches of the apple tree. We said our vows under the tree and under the gaze of the giant snake. Roshi Bernie Glassman and Roshi Egyoku Nakao were the officiants, and at the appropriate moment, Bernie picked apples from the tree and Shinko and I both took bites from them with our arms intertwined. We called the ceremony "A Return to Eden" that absolved the curse of original sin. As part of the service, Bernie and Egyoku performed a water purification ceremony and we purified ourselves and atoned for all of our negative karma. There is no way to defile purity. All sin and evil were wiped out. Everything is whole and complete as it is.

O

From all my early years of exposure to the sun as a lifeguard at swimming pools in Phoenix and countless hours on the beach in Southern California, the light in my eyes was starting to fade. My lenses were becoming clouded with cataracts. My ophthalmologist said I needed surgery to remove my dull lenses and insert clear plastic ones. He could even correct my vision so I would not have to wear the glasses I had worn since I was thirteen years old. The lens in one eye would focus for distance vision, and the other would focus for reading; my brain would compensate for the difference. The prospect of getting out of bed in the morning without groping for my glasses was one that thrilled and delighted me.

The surgeon makes a cut in the cornea of the eye in order to remove the defective lens and to insert a new one. There are no nerves in the eye, but the anesthesiologist is present to drip tranquilizing drugs into a patient's veins during the operation. I told both doctors that I wanted to have the surgery with no drugs since I had been a meditator for more than forty years and knew how to keep calm. The anesthesiologist was skeptical, but we agreed that he could insert a needle in my vein and if my blood pressure or heart rate rose, he could inject his drugs.

I spent the operation focusing my attention on my eye, the scalpel, and the surgeon. Everything was out of focus, but it was an interesting light show. I survived the operations on both eyes without drugs, and the surgeon and the anesthesiologist were most impressed. The best part was that I was not doped up and could carry on with the activities of my life without taking time to recover. With my bionic eyes, I saw the world in a new light.

The surgeon started asking me questions about meditation and told me that he was going to start sitting with me. He never showed up. Nonetheless, it was a big effort to entice one person toward meditation.

○

Meditation has been in the media lately, especially the Buddhist-based Mindfulness Meditation—the practice of cultivating a nonjudgmental awareness of the present moment.

Studies have shown that meditation can reduce stress, lower blood pressure, and help one's general health and well-being. I had always assumed that if everyone meditated, social and political conflict would end. That is not to say that there have been no conflicts within the walls of Zen monasteries, but Buddhist lore states that compassion is the natural outcome of the insight that comes through meditation. Compassion is the functioning of wisdom. I had claimed that only good would arise if the president of the United States and the cabinet meditated. Then there was a case that challenged my claim.

The former governor of South Carolina, Mark Sanford, was disgraced after it was discovered that he was using state funds to carry on an extramarital affair with a lover in South America. After leaving office, Sanford learned about Mindfulness Meditation and practiced it almost daily. It gave him the confidence to reenter the political arena, and in 2013 he was elected as a South Carolina member of the U.S. House of Representatives. Before starting to meditate, Sanford had political views that seemed devoid of compassion. For instance, he refused federal money that would have helped the plight of the poor in his state. After meditating for three years, his political views did not change. They still seemed to be devoid of compassion. I was quite discouraged to read about him in the media and felt I had to reassess my view that meditation would bring only positive consequences for society.

At that time there was an explosion of articles in national publications about how meditation can help you get the competitive edge in your business or learn to study better and get better grades or to be more productive at work. There was nothing about being a better person with concerns about the welfare of all people. To many of us in the Buddhist community, this seemed like a perversion of the original teachings and intent of the Buddha.

My faith was restored by a study funded by the nonprofit Mind and Life Institute. Thirty-nine people who had never meditated before completed eight weeks of meditation training. Then their "level of compassion" was tested.

Two actors sat in a staged waiting area with three chairs. The participant, who sat in the third chair, was told that the experiment was testing memory and cognitive ability; but really, researchers were testing what happened when another actor, a woman, appeared who was using crutches and wearing a walking boot and seemed to be in pain. Since all three chairs were occupied, she leaned against the wall, wincing.

The actors ignored her; would the meditator act compassionately and give up the chair for the suffering person?

Researcher David DeSteno wrote in the *New York Times* that "the results were striking":

> Although only 16 percent of the nonmeditators gave up their seats—an admittedly disheartening fact—the proportion rose to 50 percent among those who had meditated. This increase is impressive not solely because it occurred after only eight weeks of meditation, but also because it did so within the context of a situation known to inhibit considerate behavior: witnessing others ignoring a person in distress—what psychologists call the bystander effect—reduces the odds that any single individual will help. Nonetheless, the meditation increased the compassionate response threefold. ("The Morality of Meditation," July 5, 2013)

In conversations with Sean Murphy, one of my students, he came up with the idea of developing an institute that trains meditation teachers. These teachers would not be fully certified Zen teachers but would be able to instruct others in the basics of meditation. I enthusiastically supported him and his colleagues, who created the Sage Institute in Taos, New Mexico. The institute, as stated on its web site, "supports the promotion and practice of all forms of meditation and mindfulness. We offer trainings in mindfulness, and also trainings to teach people how to teach mindfulness in their own communities. We believe in consciousness, creativity, and meditation as vehicles for personal and political transformation in our world."

The past several decades have witnessed an explosion of yoga instructors who know the basic postures but who are not trained in the spiritual aspects of the practice. Yoga has penetrated the board room and the school room. We would like to see nonsectarian meditation promulgated in a similar fashion.

One of the criticisms of this program is that it waters down the original teachings of the Buddha and is not self-sustaining unless there is rigorous training. I have reflected quite a bit on this point and have once again come to the conclusion that the more people who meditate, the better for individuals, their communities, and the global community. In the history of Zen, hundreds of thousands of monks have embarked on the Buddha Way. However, only a handful have deeply realized the Buddha Dharma and have transmitted the profound teachings. There was Hui-Neng, the Sixth Patriarch in China, who became enlightened hearing a sutra chanted in the marketplace. Master Joshu started his practice as a young teenager and had considerable insight at an early age. He lived and taught until he was more than one hundred years old. Dogen Zenji had great doubt as a young man and took a dangerous journey in the thirteenth century from Japan to China in search of an authentic teacher. He returned to Japan and founded the Soto school there and left a legacy of Zen writings that are still studied and revered by the current generation of Zen students. Hakuin revitalized Rinzai Zen in Japan. He entered the Way before his tenth birthday because of his fear of burning in Hell.

The heads of these venerable Zen masters and some others poked up above the crowd. I see that the same thing will happen now. I view the community of Zen teachers as a collective that is spreading seeds, watering the soil, and providing nutrients and sunlight. Every once in a while a great plant will grow. It could be one of my students or the student of one of my Dharma relatives or a student in some distant lineage. Such superior students will carry on the profound, mysterious tradition, and the vast ocean of meditators will support those efforts and live their lives in service of peace, harmony, and wellness.

We never know all of the conditions that give rise to the consequences in each of our lives. However, with the advancement of meditation through all realms of society, we will move closer to the goal of a peaceful world.

○

In 2010 Shinko and I started an annual trip to Madrid, Spain. Shinko grew up in Madrid from the age of ten when her mother moved there from Puerto Rico. She is a *madrileña*. The *madrileños,* those who are of or from Madrid, are her people. When we started teaching Zen in Madrid, the students responded to her in a way they never did in the United States. She finally could fully express herself as a Zen teacher without push-back.

Shinko's mother was living in Madrid, and our original impetus was to visit her regularly as she grew older. We met some Zen students there and started giving public talks and then leading workshops and retreats in the city and its environs. We now have a small dedicated sangha that meets at Kay Zen, a retreat center on the outskirts of Madrid in the ancient town of El Escorial.

At first I did not like Madrid. It was another large, dirty, crowded, noisy city. I preferred to get out of the city to visit the ancient walled towns of Avila or Toledo or to go to the coast to Alicante or Barcelona. One of Shinko's sisters lives in Barcelona, and their mother, who was recently widowed, is moving to Barcelona to be near the sister. We will continue to use Barcelona as an embarkation point to some of the Mediterranean islands. Over the years we visited the Spanish island of Mallorca, the Italian island of Sardinia, and the French island of Corsica. We both love the water and always try to spend some time near the sea or the ocean.

Speaking in Madrid, 2010

Over time I began to appreciate what Madrid has to offer. Shinko's mother lived close to the center of town, and every day I took a walk and explored the parks, monuments, museums, markets, and narrow streets of the old town. I had lived in many large cities in my life, including Los Angeles, San Francisco, San Diego, Mexico City, and London. When I was younger, I reveled in the excitement that a large city has to offer. Now as I am older, I prefer the quiet rural life. But Madrid gave me the opportunity to keep stepping into the unknown. Isn't tomorrow an unknown even if we stay put in a place where we know the traditions and every piece of ground is familiar? It is much more so when I am in a foreign country where I struggle with the language.

During our third trip to Madrid, we connected with a small number of students who were hungry for the Dharma. They particularly resonated with Shinko's passion for the Dharma. Through the Internet we are able to continue our teachings with them throughout the year and continue it through retreats when we travel to Madrid. Even with the poor economy and the Spanish unemployment rate being one of the highest in the developed world, or maybe because of it, the Spanish are eager to embrace the ancient path of the Buddha.

As I reflect on my life in my seventy-fourth year, the abiding theme has been to reveal my original self and to share it with others. My search has taken me down the path blazed by the Buddha and adapted by my Japanese ancestors. One stated goal of Buddhist practice is to become unconditioned and freshly open to each situation as it arises. We are all conditioned by our environments. My Japanese teachers were all deeply conditioned by their culture, and I am sure that all of my American Zen colleagues and I are also conditioned by our American culture. In spite of this, we all have taken the same precepts and do our best under the circumstances.

At each major transition on my path, I have reaffirmed my commitment to my vows and the three pure precepts: to cease doing evil, to do good, and to do good for others. These precepts are the functioning of the three treasures of Buddha,

Dharma, and Sangha. To cease doing evil does not necessarily mean living a life of purity and chastity. It means living a life in constant contact with impermanence and with the boundless space of the indefinable and ungraspable absolute. It means to maintain a mind of "not-knowing," to be as unconditioned as possible. The Buddha treasure is wisdom of the emptiness of self and all things. Emptiness means "devoid of any fixed quality." When something is fixed or permanent, it is knowable, but it is limited and incomplete. When we maintain a mind of not-knowing, all possibilities exist.

Doing good helps us identify which of the many possibilities will alleviate suffering in ourselves and others. Doing good means fully engaging each situation without prejudice by bearing witness to both joys and suffering. And doing good for others affirms our interconnectedness. Whatever action we take has to be based on an open mind of not-knowing and a deep connection to the feelings of being present and bearing witness.

Ultimately there is nothing to grasp. I have entered this world empty handed, and so shall I leave it. What do I have to show for my seven decades of life? I hope I have planted a seed or two that will flower and continue to spread more seeds.

Chapter 16

BEARING WITNESS

> Kyogen pointed to a snow lion and said,
> "Can anyone go beyond this color?"
> —*Book of Equanimity* Case 26

Kyogen's white snow lion arises in the vast space of emptiness. We are so accustomed to looking at the foreground, we do not see the background. We get fixated on our reactions to praise and blame and are not aware of the space in which our reactions arise.

Dharma Master Jo said, "Heaven and earth have the same root. The ten thousand things are one body." Praise and blame have the same root. What is that root? Are you aware of the spaciousness that envelopes heaven and earth, praise and blame, the mountains and the rivers? Are you aware of the silence that drowns out the judgments and projections of your mind? The container of our life is vast and empty. Our feelings, emotions, and thoughts arise within that spaciousness. Problems arise when we forget about the space and make the objects of our perception solid and immutable. What a pity!

In 2014 Bernie and Egyoku started to revitalize the Zen Peacemaker Order and asked me to be steward of the central USA circle. I had decided to join and follow the order rule, which includes the three tenets of *Not Knowing,* by giving up fixed ideas about ourselves and the universe; *Bearing Witness* to the joy and suffering of the world; and *Taking Action* that arises from Not-Knowing and Bearing Witness. It also includes the four commitments of (1) a reverence for all life, (2) a sustainable and ethical economy, (3) equal rights for all, and (4) stewardship of the Earth.

Another requirement of membership is to attend a Bearing Witness retreat, either at a place of great suffering or on city streets as a homeless person. For the past twenty years, Bernie and the Zen Peacemaker community had been leading Bearing Witness retreats at the Nazi concentration camp Auschwitz. Bernie had been holding homeless retreats on the streets of New York City for even more years. According to Bernie, too many Zen students find a comfort zone in the traditional practice and need to take a plunge into the unknown to shake up their fixed notions.

I view our Zen practice as a process of continually stepping into the unknown, or, I should say, "learning how to accept stepping into the unknown." We are always stepping into the unknown because we never know what will be arising next in our lives or even what will be the results of our actions.

I had not been able to attend an Auschwitz retreat because of scheduling and finances. But when the Zen Peacemakers announced a Native American Bearing Witness retreat in the Black Hills of South Dakota, I immediately signed up. This retreat came about through the efforts of my old Dharma buddy Grover Genro Gauntt, who over the past twelve years had visited the elders and members of the Oglala Sioux Pine Ridge Indian Reservation (Wazí Aháŋhaŋ Oyáŋke in Lakota). Genro had made deep friendships and participated in their sacred ceremonies.

In August 2015, I spent five days camping in the Black Hills at a Lakota Sioux ceremonial site to bear witness to the stories of Native Americans in the area, to visit the Pine Ridge Reservation and the Wounded Knee memorial, and to share their ceremonies. It was a most profound and inspiring event. One action that arose from that Bearing Witness is to recount some of the events, stories, and activities that affected me the most.

The history of the native people in the Americas is a history of deceit, treachery, and genocide. Native populations across what are now the fifty states of the United States were almost exterminated. The expropriation of more than two billion acres from the Atlantic to the Pacific and the deaths of fifteen million natives involved the most extensive land fraud and the largest genocide in world history. Indians today have the worst poverty levels and the shortest life expectancies of any ethnic group in the United States.

During the Bearing Witness retreat, a wide variety of Native Americans told their stories. We experienced their pain and we also shared their joy. Despite an oppressive history, those Indians who maintain their traditions find joy and solace in their ceremonies and their prayers.

I deeply resonated with the natives' respect of Mother Earth. Each morning started with a sunrise ceremony. We formed a circle while a Lakota elder chanted to the earth and the rising sun. We turned to the south, the west, the north, and the east in turn as the chant affirmed the virtues of each direction. During the chanting, I heard and saw the earth sigh and then felt and saw the earth breathing as she heaved rhythmically. Tears came to my eyes. The Sioux Nation has suffered and been traumatized so much in these Black Hills, and Mother Earth was feeling their pain.

The east represents *wisdom*. Light originates from the east in the rising sun that illuminates everything. The east also represents the spring when everything, including wisdom, grows.

The south represents *generosity*. The sun is highest in the south, and the season is summer. Summer is abundant, and we can show our appreciation by being generous, not only with material things, but also with generosity of spirit.

The west is where the sun sets and the chill of autumn returns. It represents *bravery* or *courage*—courage to face the uncertainty and the unknown as darkness sets in.

The north is winter and cold and darkness. It represents *patience* and *tolerance*. We need those virtues to transform the darkness as we wait for the eventual light in the east.

The Lakota have three more virtues that are associated with Mother Earth: *respect,* or honor; *compassion;* and *humility.* These seven virtues—wisdom, generosity, courage, patience, respect, compassion, and humility—comprise the Seven Laws of the Lakota. They are to be maintained daily. Of course it is cardinal that we treat other humans with the dignity of these seven virtues, but we should also extend them to the spirits of all creations, including insects, four-legged animals, animals that fly and swim; and to all manifestations of Mother Earth, including plants, rocks, rivers, mountains, and fire.

During the weeklong retreat a sacred fire burned continuously in the center of the ceremonial circle. A friend, Grant Couch, and I volunteered to be fire guardians from 1 to 3 a.m. each night. I had recently read that ancient peoples often divided their sleep in two parts and were up for a few hours in the middle of the night during what is called the "hour of God."

At that deep part of the night there were no lights other than from the fire and the brilliant stars. The Milky Way was a river in the heavens. We saw numerous shooting stars each night.

I usually spent the first hour connecting with the spirit of the fire. Fire is a shape shifter and has the potential to rage out of control. But it is clear that the spirit of fire comes from Mother Earth. Everything comes from Mother Earth without exception: the food we eat, the water we drink, the air we breathe. Automobiles, computers, designer clothes, roof tiles, electricity, and granite countertops all come from Mother Earth. When we do not adequately respect and honor her and have compassion for all of her creations, we lose our connection and begin to exploit her.

The role of ancestors is very important to Native Americans. During ceremonies, they pray to the spirits of their ancestors for guidance and protection. The Lakota Sioux have inhabited the sacred sites of the area for hundreds of generations. The presence of their ancestors is palpable. I could feel their spirits rising from the ground, the trees, the grasses; I could feel them in the sky. They were present in all of the natural settings—particularly when we visited the site of the 1890 Wounded Knee massacre.

All four of my grandparents fled to the United States to escape the persecution of the Cossacks in Eastern Europe. They came to the "Land of Opportunity" from a village in present-day Belarus. I had thought that I and my ancestors did not have much to do with the domination of the American Indians, but our opportunity came at the expense of those who lived here before us.

Three of my grandparents died before I was born. Both of my maternal grandparents committed suicide. My grandfather killed himself after the 1929 stock market crash; my grandmother jumped from the roof of a convalescent home.

When I was in my first year, my father joined the Air Force as soon as the United States entered World War II. We moved from the family home in Wisconsin to Nevada, so I don't have memories of my only living grandparent, my father's father, from that time. But we visited him when I was ten years old. Grandpa was a little old foreign man. His wife, who was the sister of his first wife, was toothless and smelled bad. I found the odor of their house to be unpleasant—probably from the food they cooked and the liniment they rubbed on themselves. They died a few years later; that was the only time I saw them.

Since my parents moved west from Wisconsin, I did not grow up around any cousins and don't really know them. Some uncles visited us; they are the only ancestors I feel any connection to. At this point, I feel that my ancestors need my prayers for their healing more than I need their protection and guidance.

I have maintained close contact with my siblings, and we regularly gather to share our lives. All of my siblings have been supportive of my Zen practice, and both Barry and Alan have attended programs at the Great Mountain Zen Center. Barbara has always been available when I needed support. They all have pursued the spiritual paths that spoke to them. I consider my siblings to be my true ancestors.

○

My family moved to Phoenix, Arizona, in 1952 when I turned eleven. An Indian boarding school stood at the corner of Central Avenue and Indian School Road. I knew nothing of what went on inside that structure, but every time we passed it, I had an ominous feeling. The area surrounding the boarding school seemed mysterious and had dark energy.

Much later I learned that Indian children were forcibly

taken from their families and Indian school administrators did their best to destroy the Indian culture. Children who spoke their native languages were beaten. They were stripped of their native clothes and taught that the ceremonies of their parents were "devil worship." They were forced to learn the tenets of Christianity. The children were indoctrinated to the ways of the U.S. consumer.

The Indian boarding schools destroyed the fabric of the Indian family structure. Before the introduction of these schools, grandparents and elders taught the young ones within the context of extended families. With the break in familial continuity, the practice of and respect for the old ways diminished, and alcoholism and abusive behavior took their place. Today, many of the Indians on reservations are traumatized, and there is a high incidence of addiction and suicide.

I often neglected my own children as I pursued my "path to enlightenment." I know that I was not a perfect father, but I always tried to be available for my children when they needed me. They have all turned out to be decent and responsible people. So either because of my influence or despite it, they managed to turn out okay. I am most grateful for their tolerance of my peripatetic ways and for their loving spirits.

Both Sam and Lily have children of their own. In the fall of 2015 I have five grandchildren, with a sixth on the way. Even though I have had difficulty looking back at the line of my ancestors, I can look forward along the stream of my progeny. Now I am in the role of ancestor and prepared to offer whatever guidance and protection I can.

O

Devout Native Americans pray to the Great Creator for the well-being of their people. They pray continuously in ceremony and throughout the day. Their cosmology is, of course, different from that of Christianity. But on the Pine Ridge Reservation a high proportion of the Indians practice Christianity.

The Sioux name for the Great Creator, Wakan Tanka, literally means "Great Mystery." Now many Indians use the word "God." They pray to God, to Mother Earth, to Father Sky, and to their ancestors. I knew little about how to pray. I did not learn from my parents or from my religious training in the Jewish synagogue or from my Zen Buddhist training. I mostly learned from Shinko, who was schooled by Catholic nuns in Puerto Rico and Madrid. Shinko and I modified the original Prayer for Peace that she wrote after 9/11. While guarding the sacred fire at the retreat in South Dakota, I chanted this prayer for an hour each night:

> All enlightened ones of the universe, bodhisattvas, protectors of the Dharma
> Together with planets, stars, and all sentient ones,
> We open our hearts to transform the five poisons of
> Ignorance, attachment, pride, envy, and anger.
> May healing, love, and peace prevail through the whole earth and entire universe.
> *Maha Prajna Paramita.*

Bodhisattvas are realized beings who dedicate themselves to the liberation of all other beings. The *Dharma* is the Truth. *Maha* means so big that there is no outside. *Prajna* is Wisdom, and *Paramita* is an aspect of an enlightened person. It literally means "crossing to the other shore." *Maha Prajna Paramita* is the Great Wisdom that takes us from the shore of suffering to

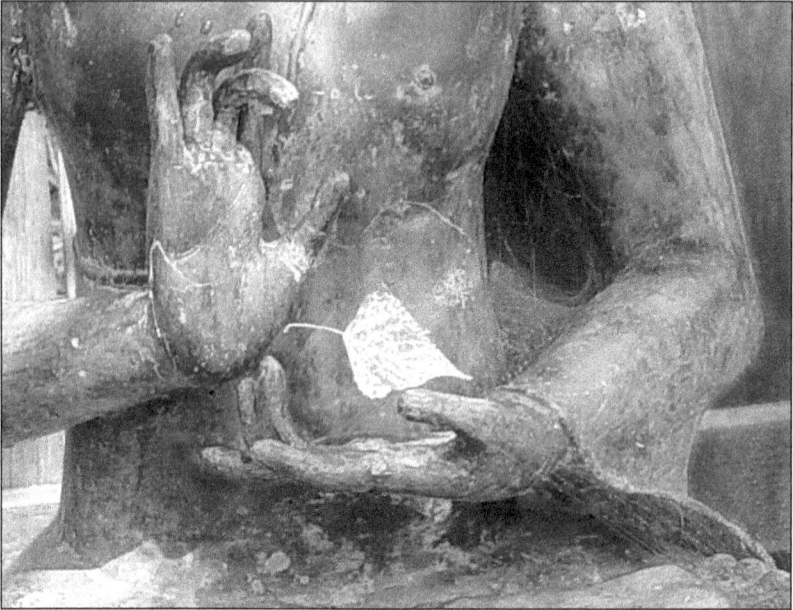

Buddha's hands with levitating leaf

the shore of enlightenment. It is a way of saying "Amen."

There is so much divisiveness in the world; we need all of the prayers for peace we can get. The problem is that we are held captive by the five poisons of ignorance, attachment, pride, envy, and anger. How do we "go beyond this color" that highlights the differences between people and causes individuals and nations to become alienated? In my travels through the years, I have met many good-hearted people of all persuasions who yearn for peace and a sustainable environment. The hard part is being able to bear witness to how each one of us contributes to hostilities and exploitation of Mother Earth. Bearing witness means being totally present without any judgments. It requires Not Knowing. It is not easy.

As I wrote more than ten years ago in *The Book of Equanimity*: "By honoring this 'not knowing' instead of fighting it, we can discover new possibilities in the midst of our problems. When we think we know all the answers, we feel safe. But life is not safe. We are all going to die. Life is a journey into the unknown."

When enough people are willing to use meditation to take a deep look at themselves while maintaining the Zen Peacemaker tenets, we will reach a critical mass of people that starts to tip the scales so that the five poisons are transformed into the five virtues of patience, generosity, humility, equanimity, and compassion. And then we will begin to see the appropriate action that needs to be taken, based on Not Knowing and Bearing Witness.

What is that number of people needed to bring about this collective awakening? I don't know. I teach one person at a time. One becomes two, and two become many. As I told my Mexican students thirty-five years ago: "Poco a poco, se va lejos." Little by little, one goes a long way.

Siblings then (1973, at Barbara's wedding): Me, Barbara, Barry, and Alan

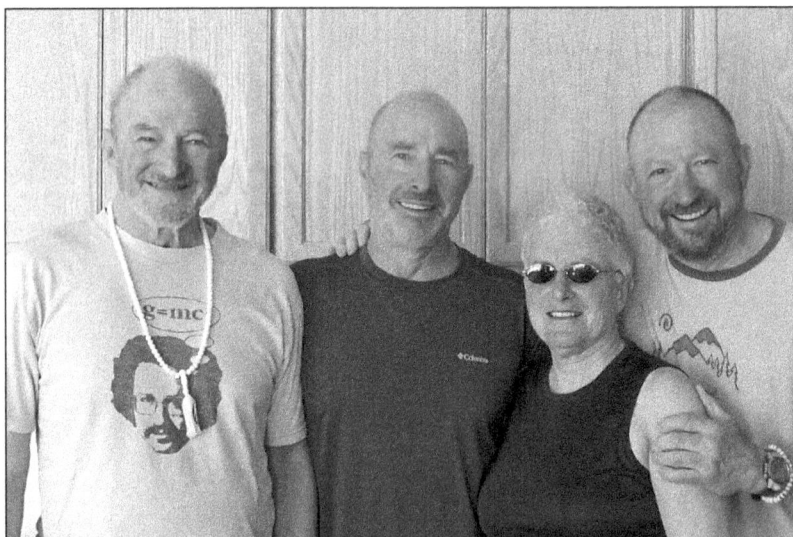

Siblings now (2014): Alan, 75; Barry, 68; Barbara, 68; and me, 73

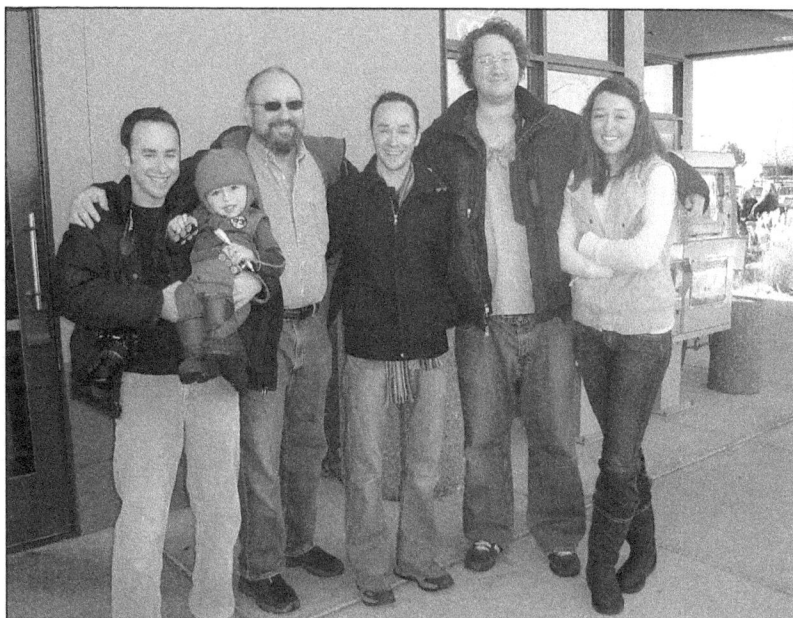

Sam holding Cooper (my first grandchild), me, David, Dan, and Lily, 2007

Me with my grandchildren (*left to right*): Logan, Poppy, Asha, Aven, and Cooper, 2015